ANTI-STRESS

COLORING BOOK

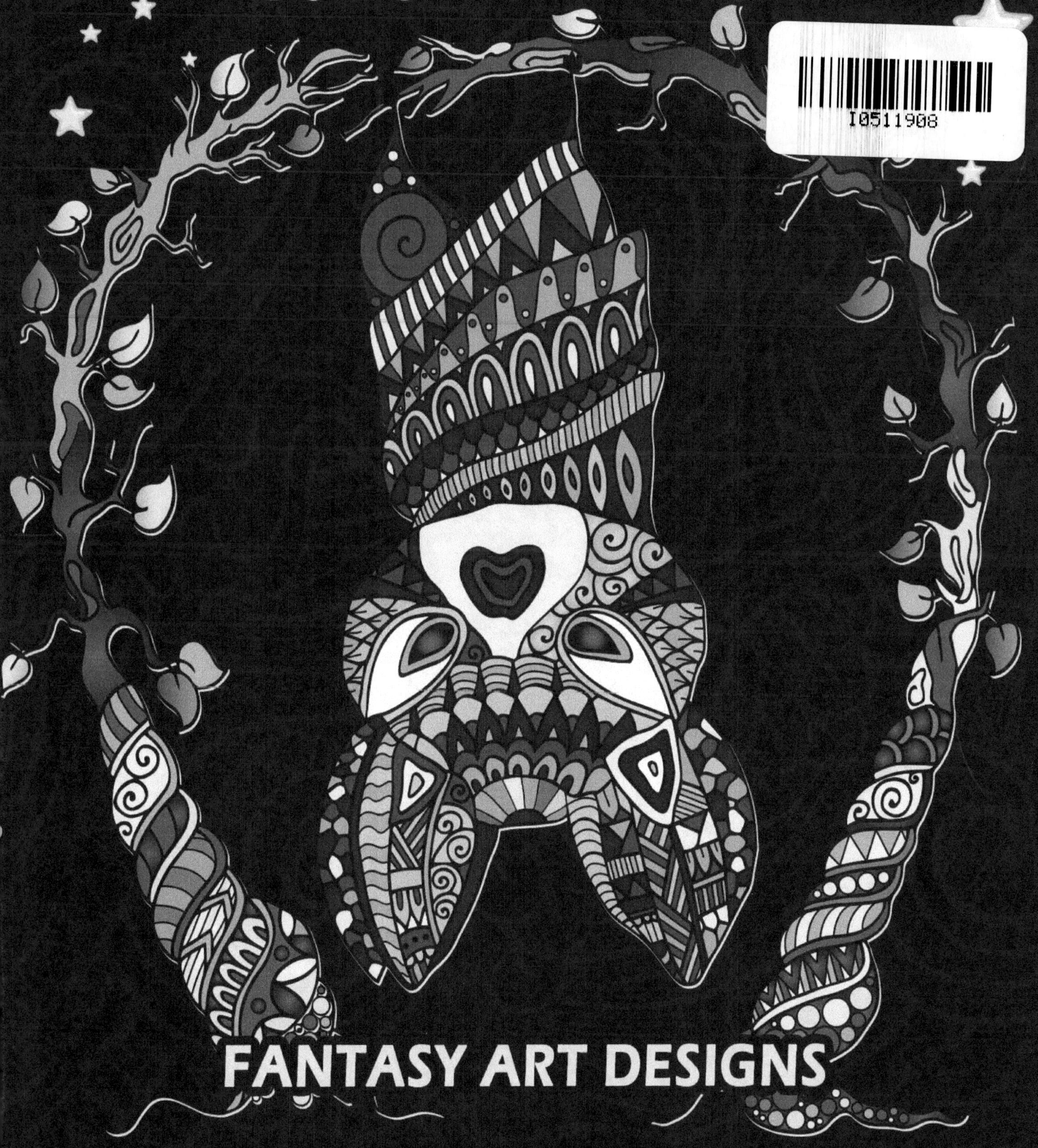

FANTASY ART DESIGNS

PUBLISHED IN 2018 BY
KODOMO PUBLISHING

PRINTED IN THE UNITED STATES OF AMERICA

COLOR TEST PAGE

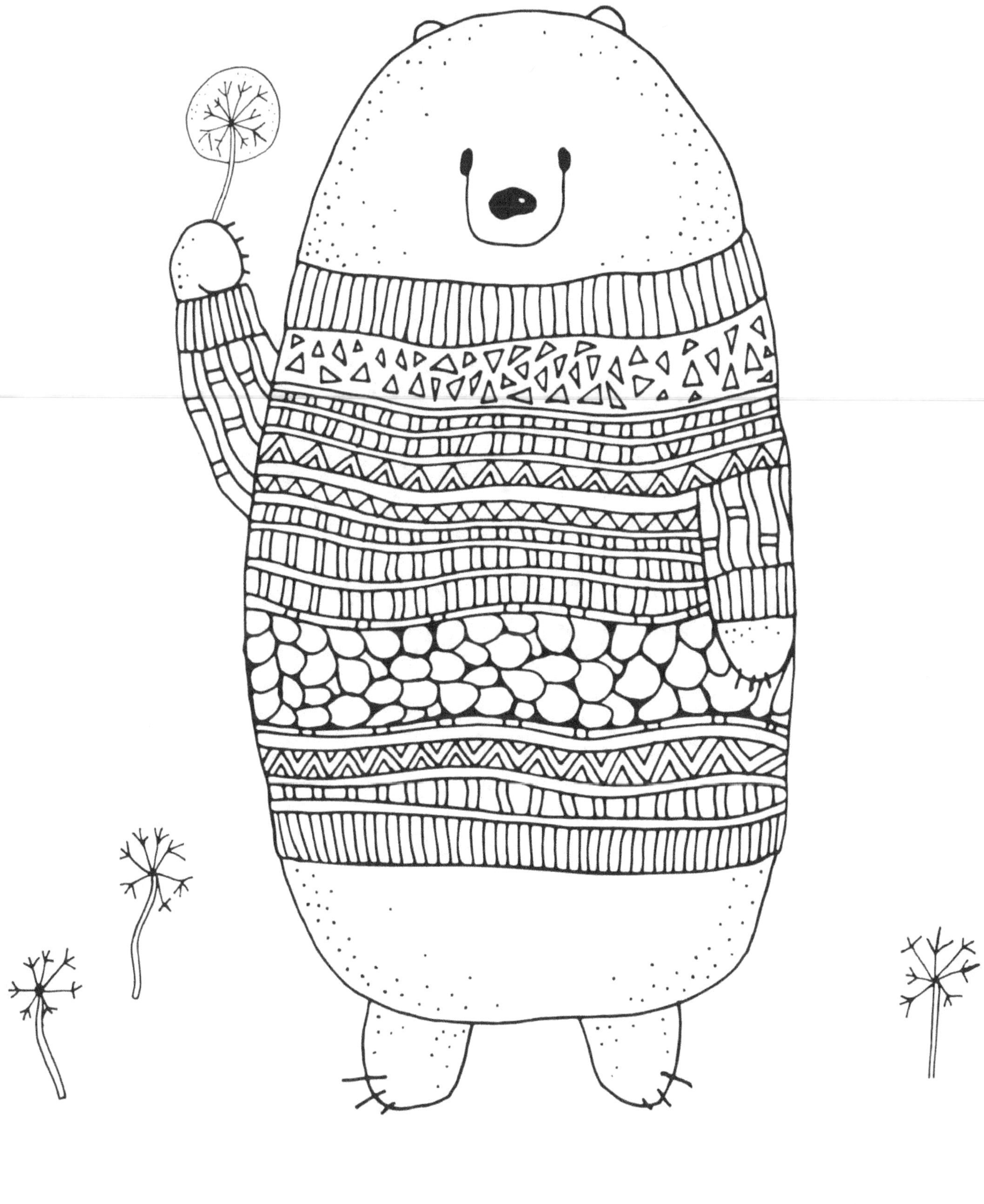

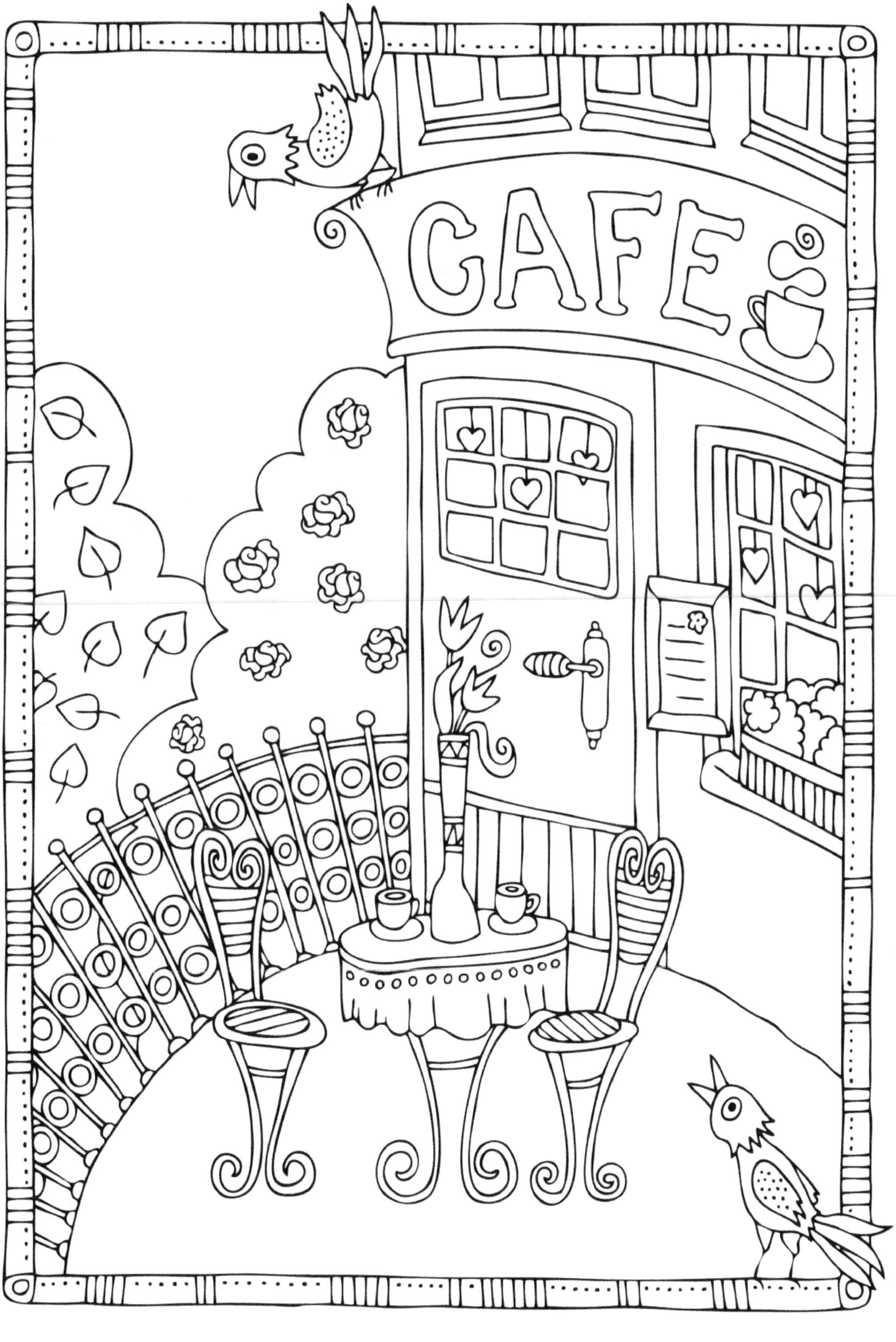
CAFE

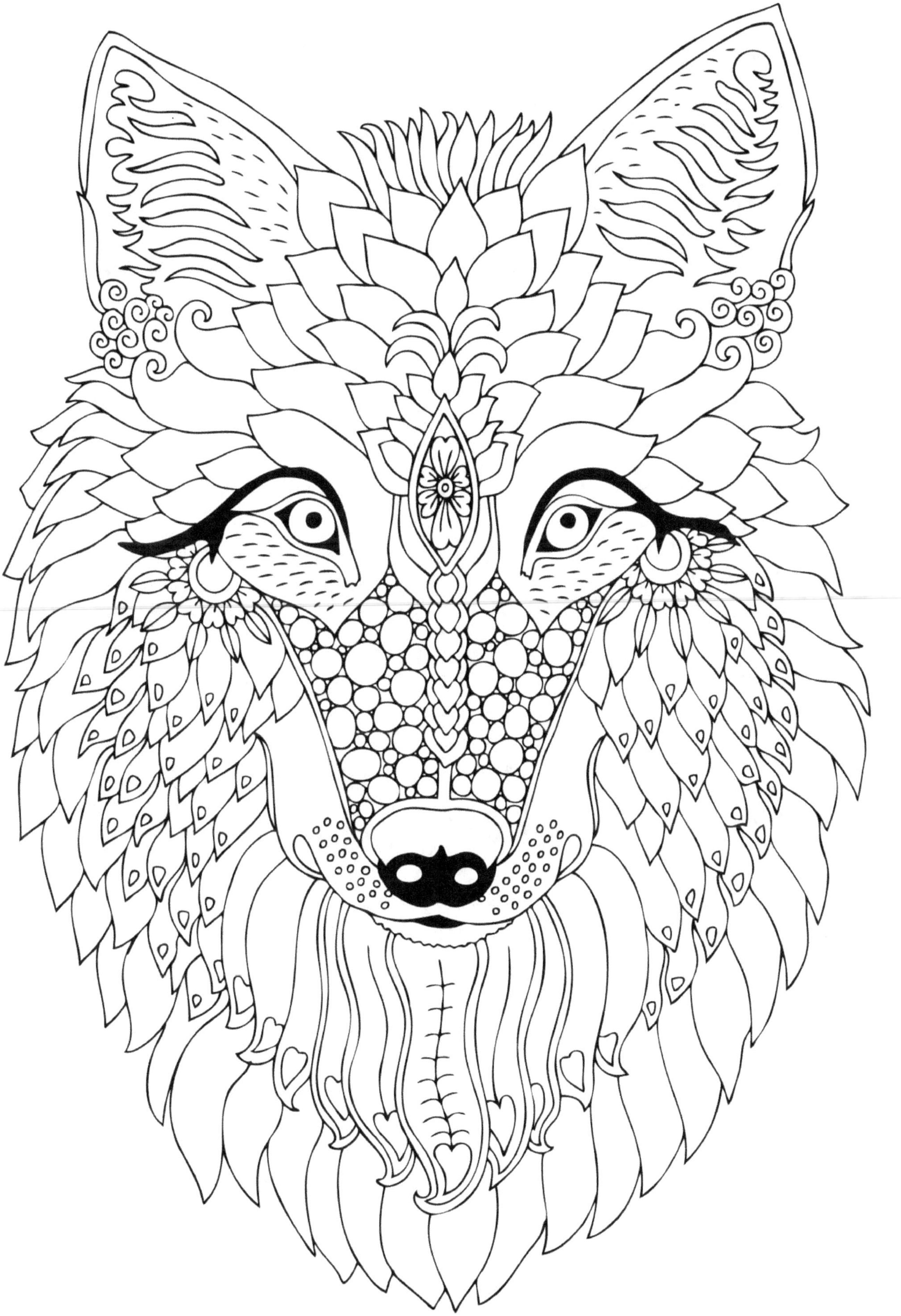

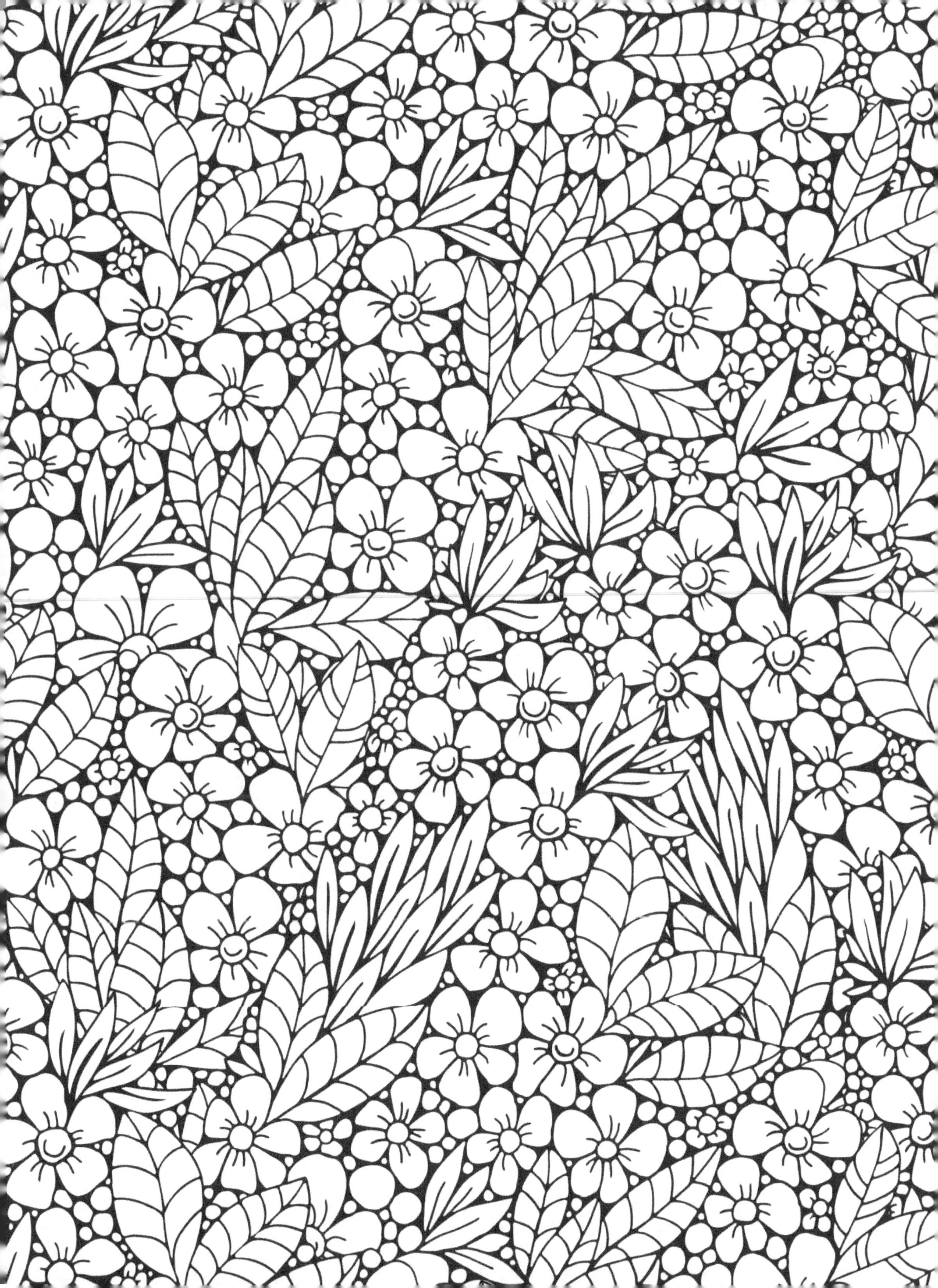

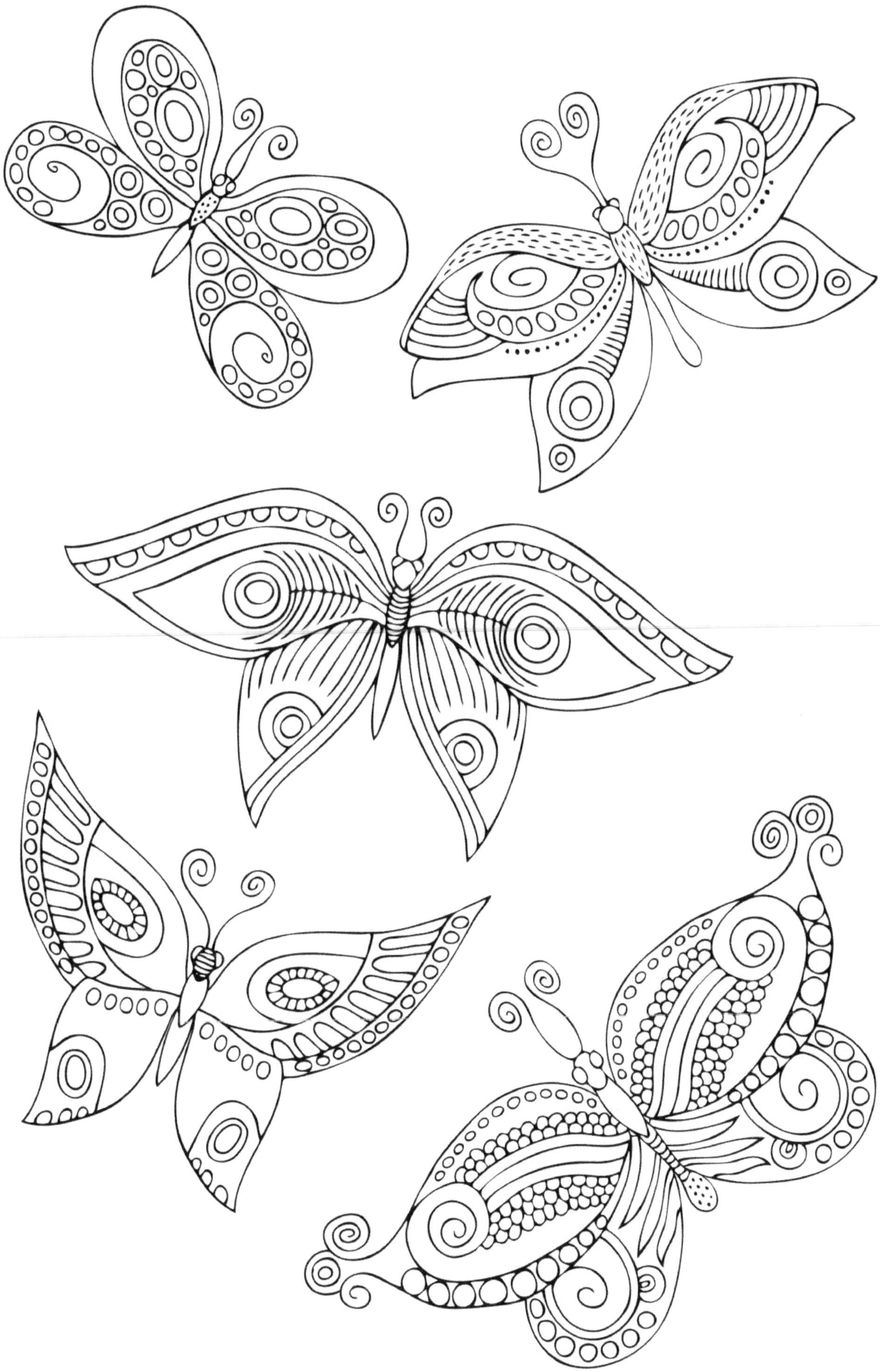

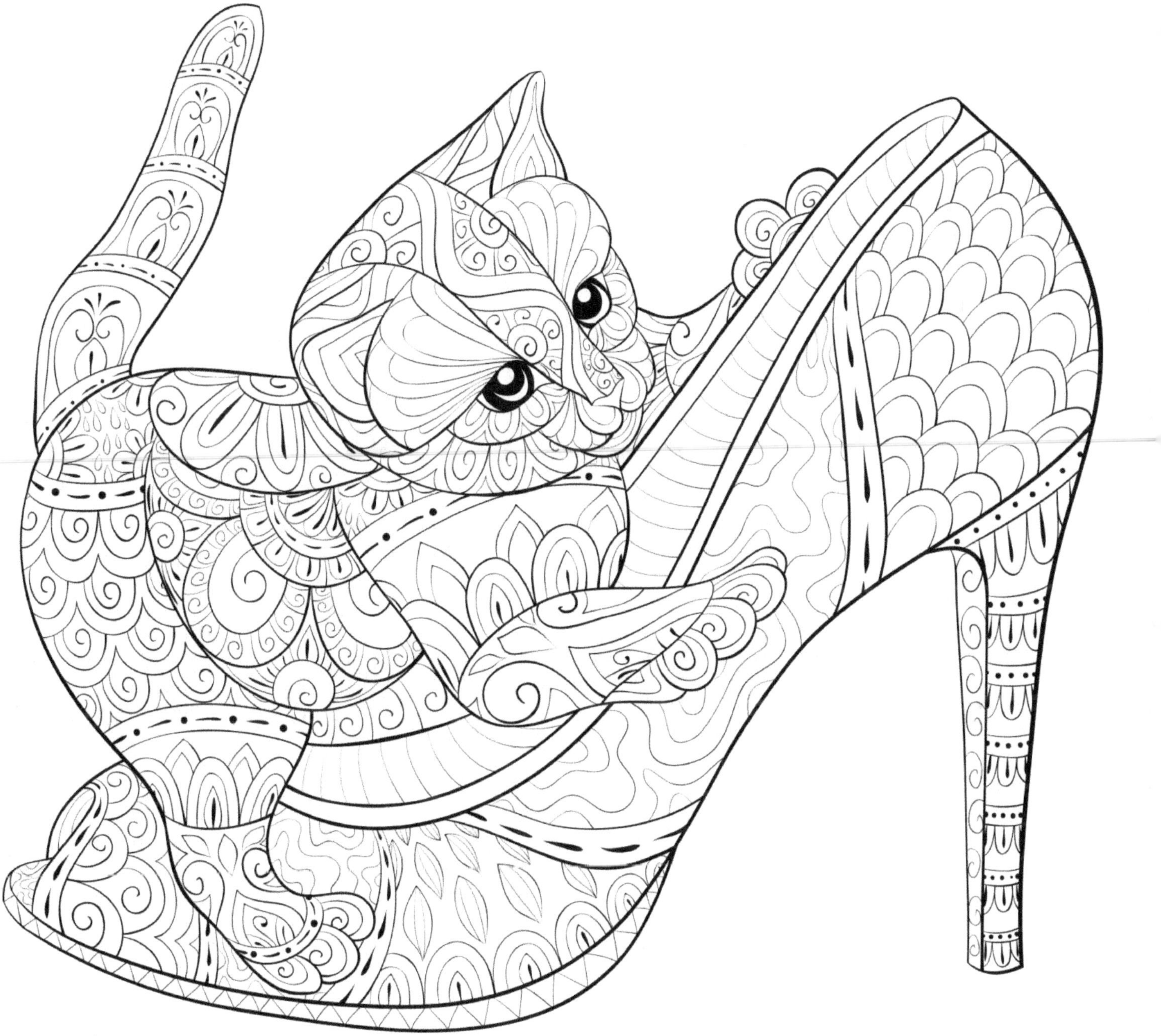

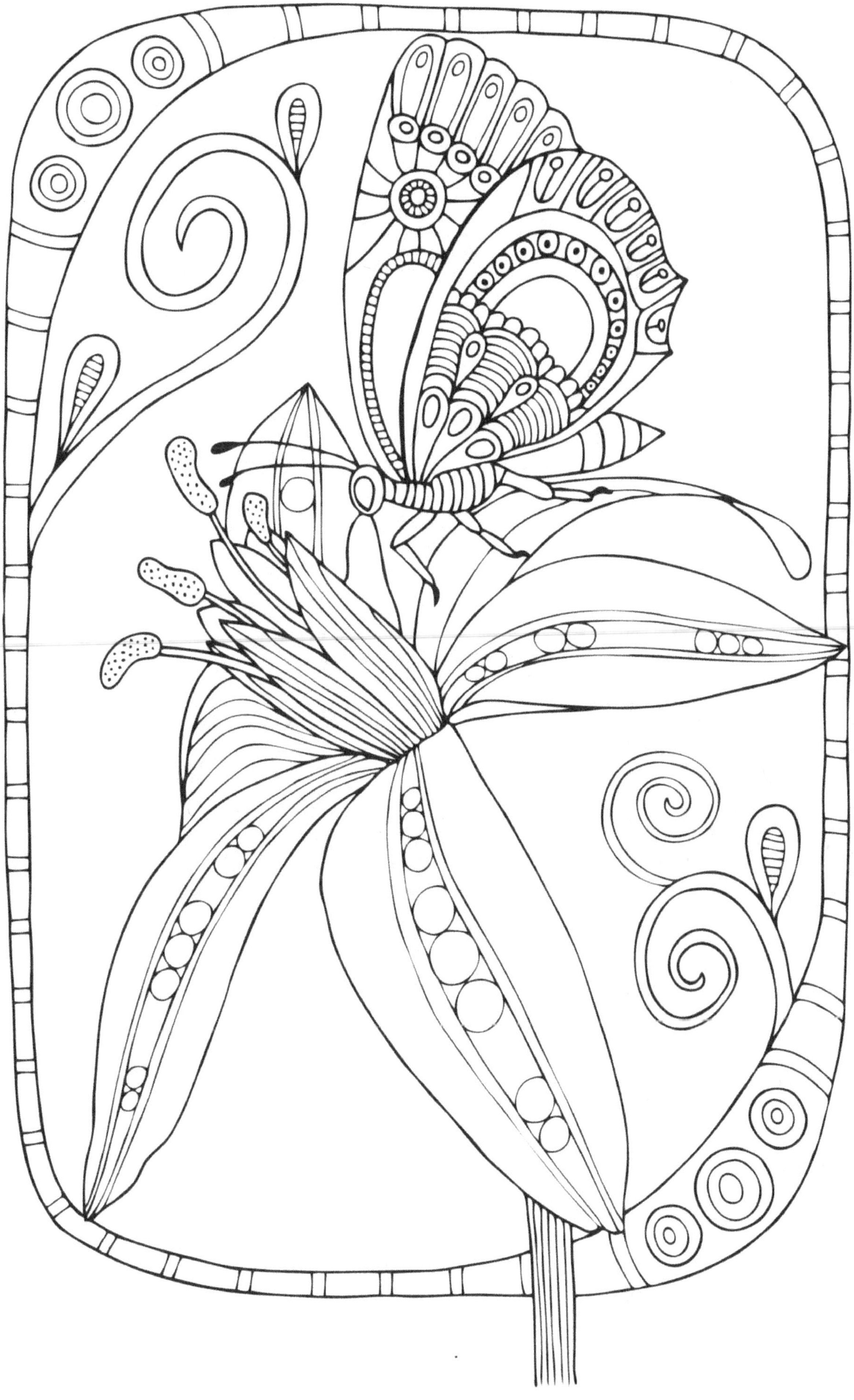

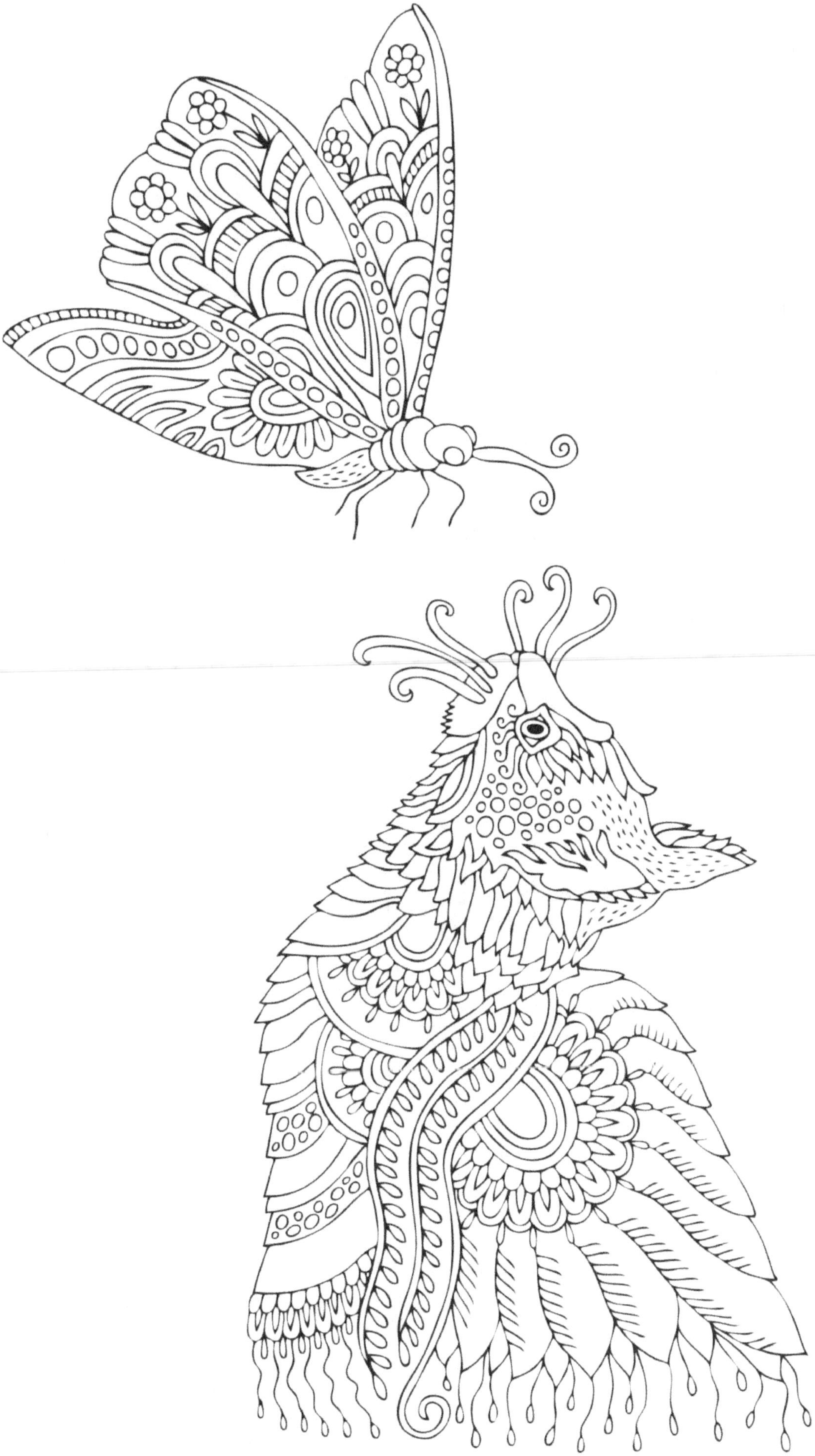

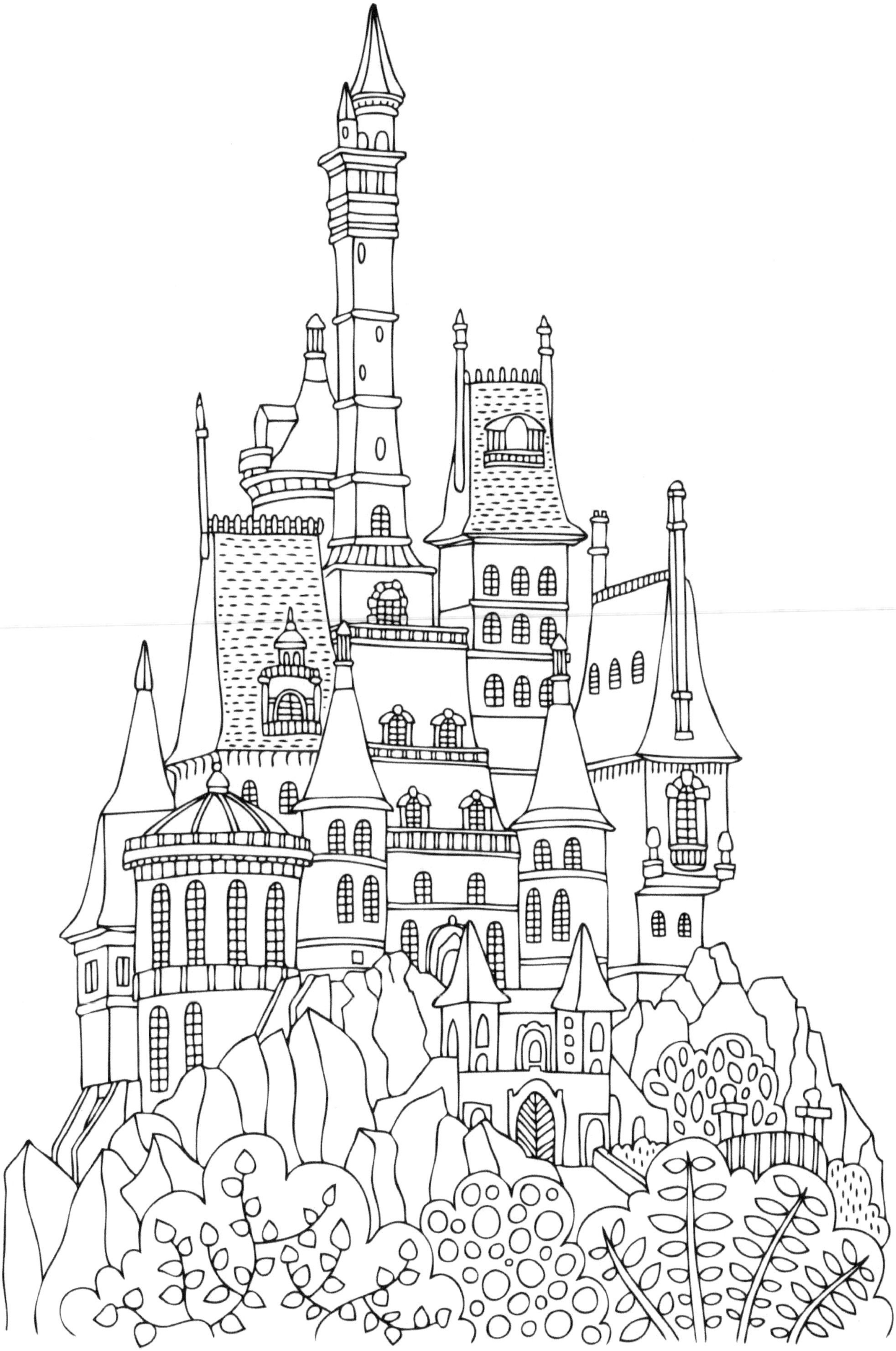

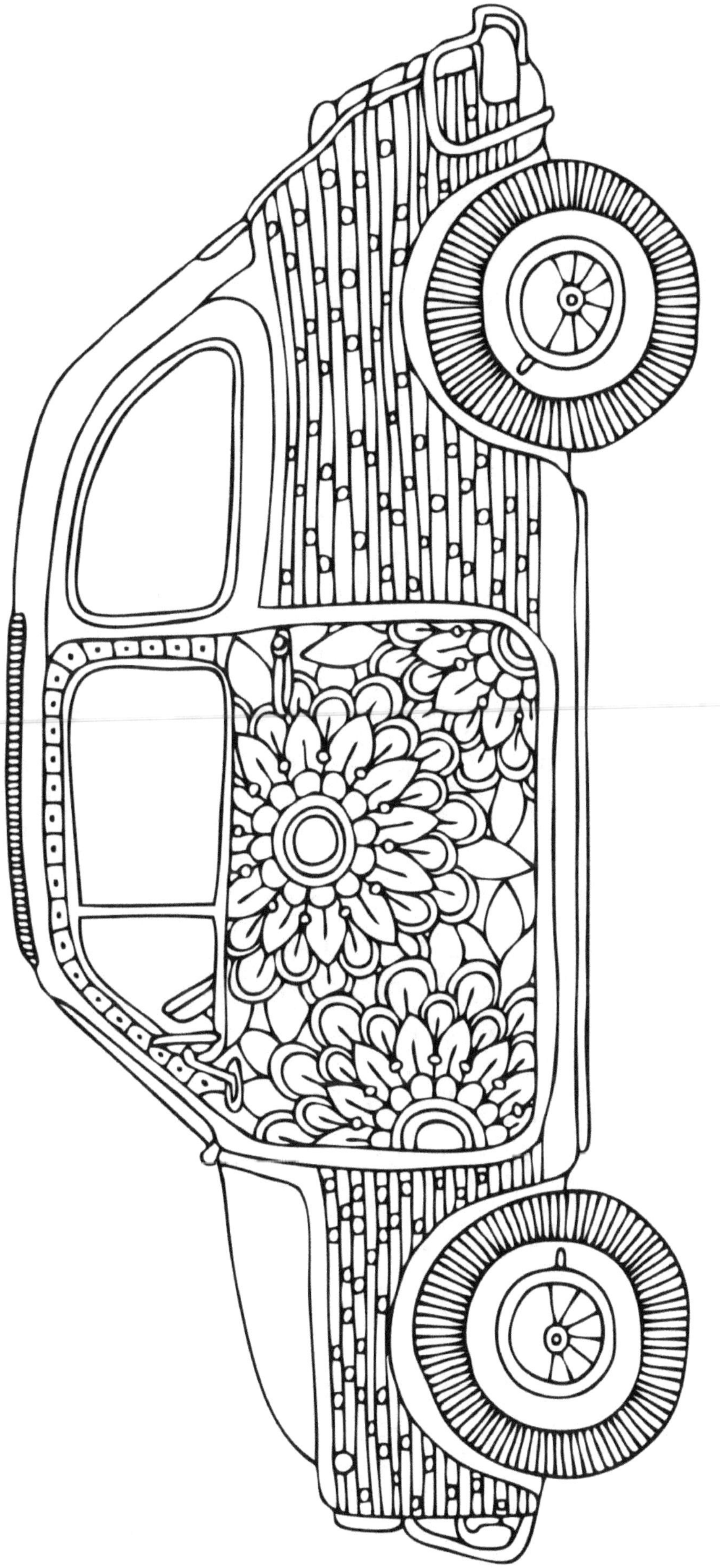

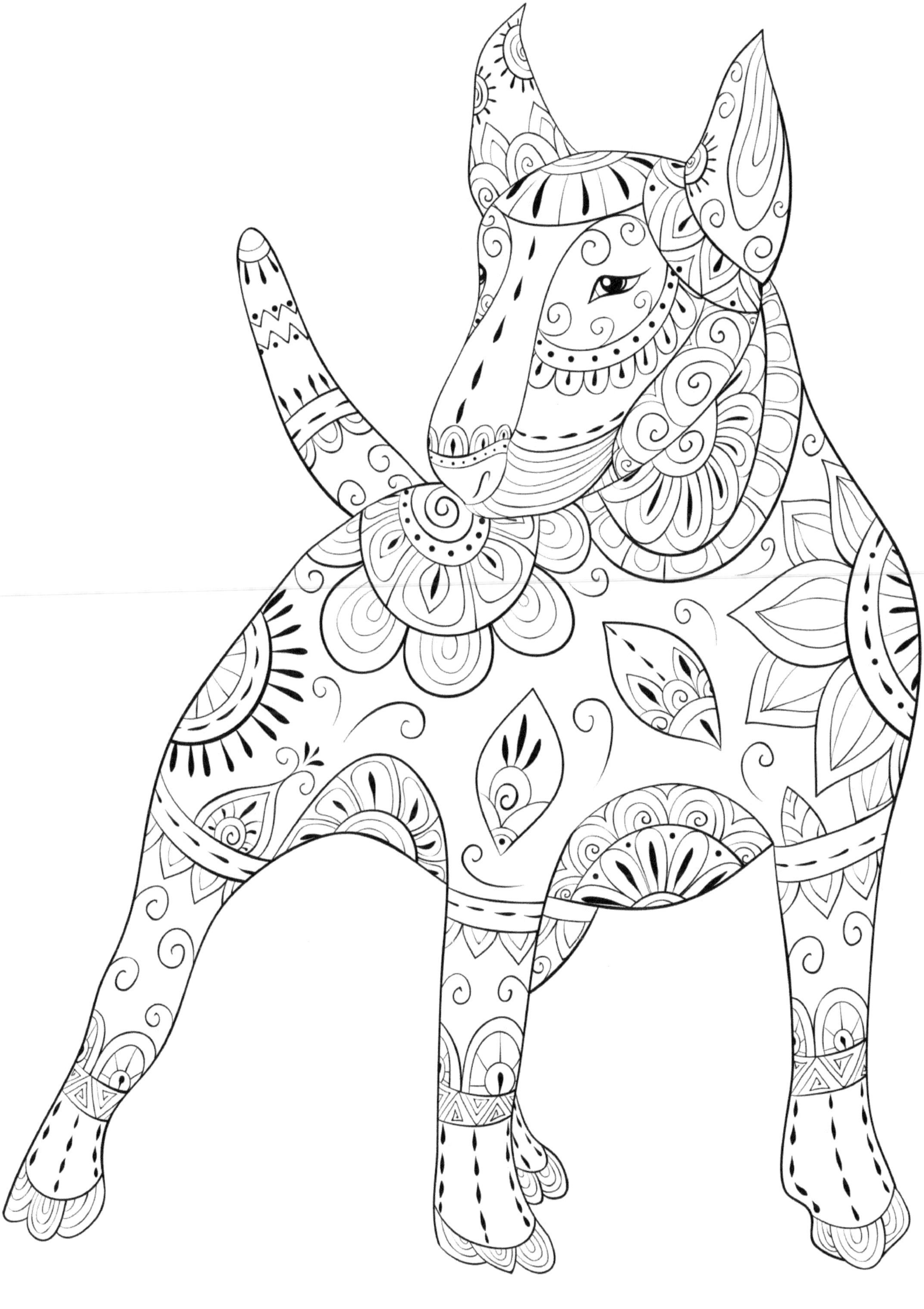

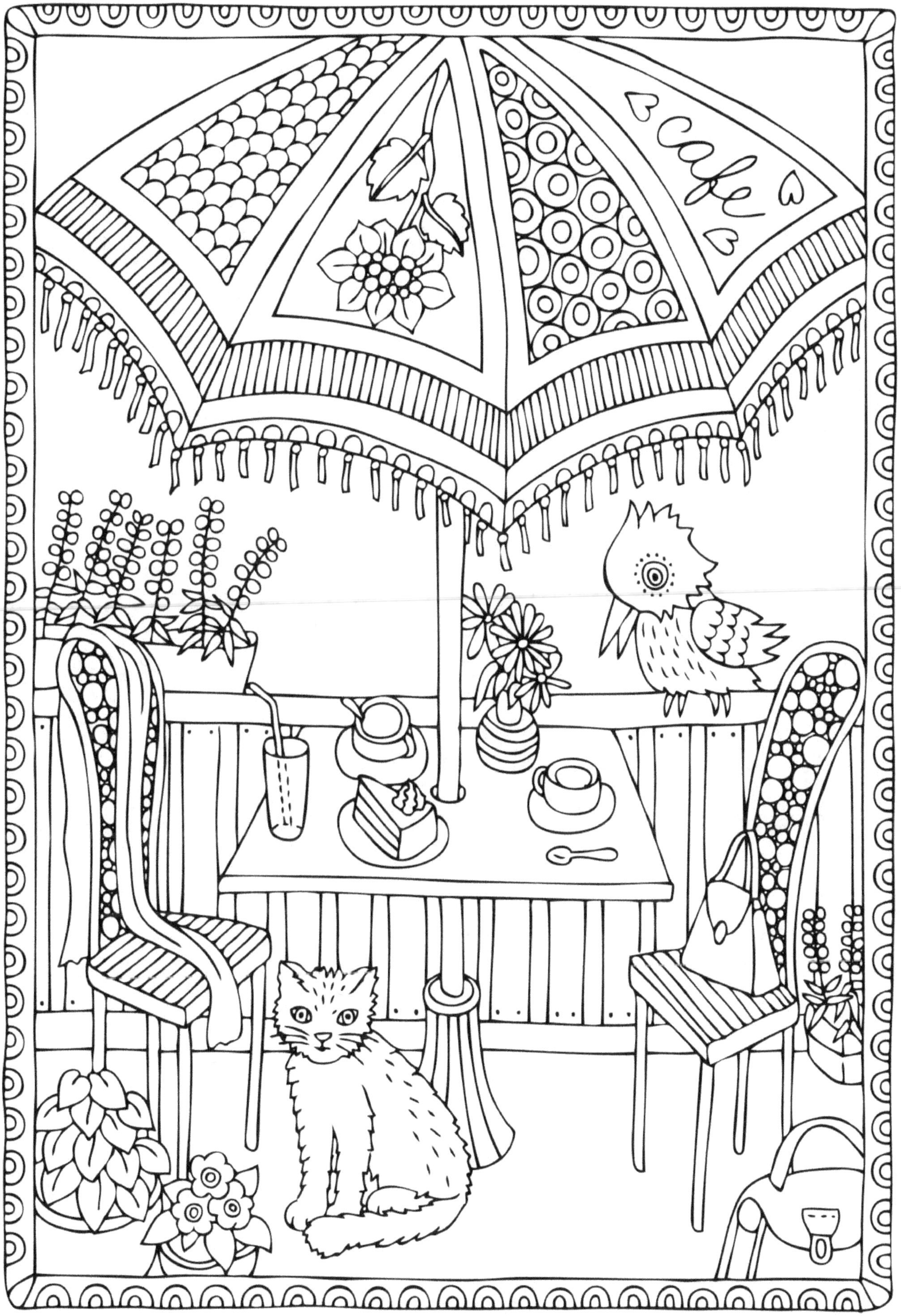
cafe

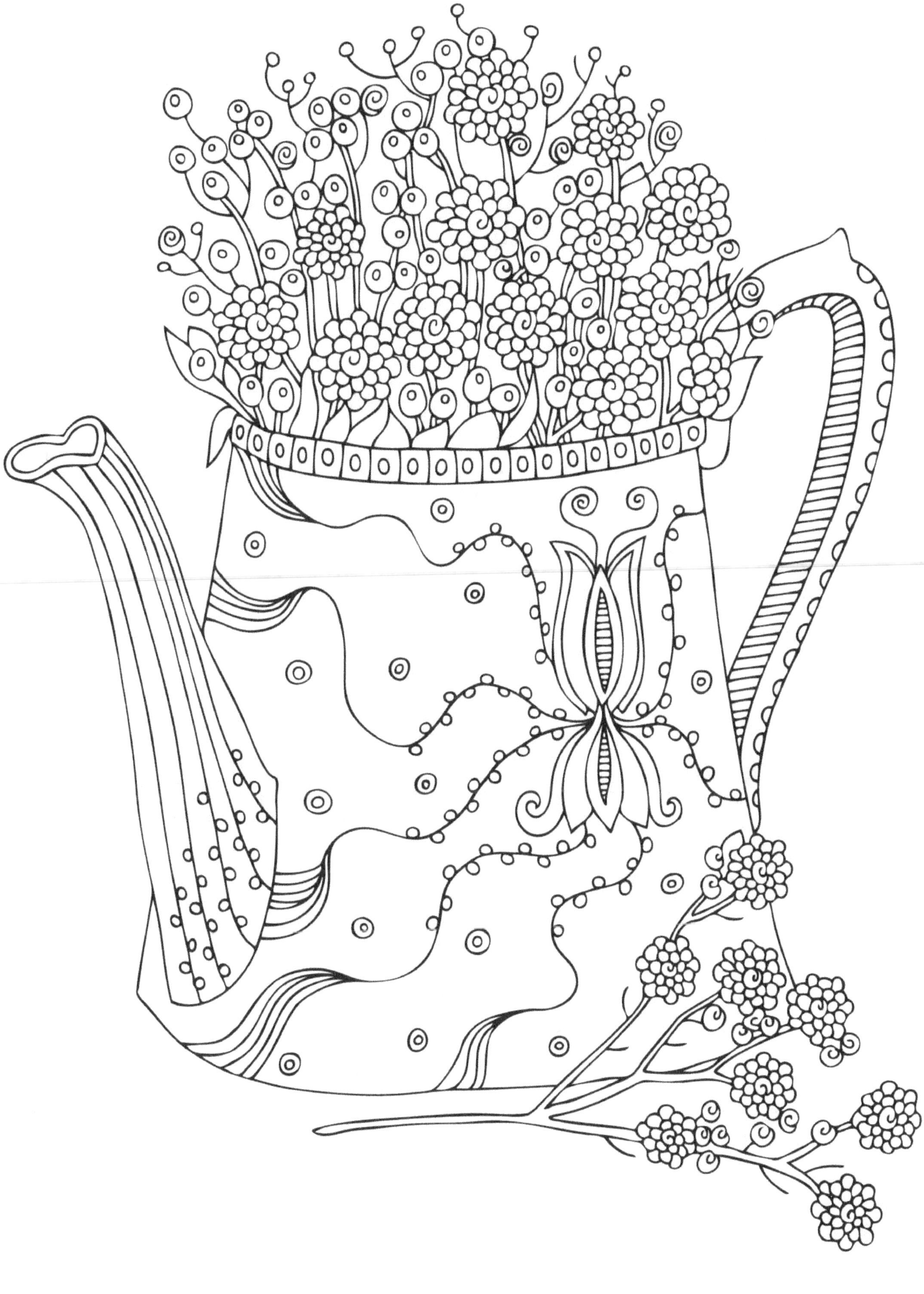

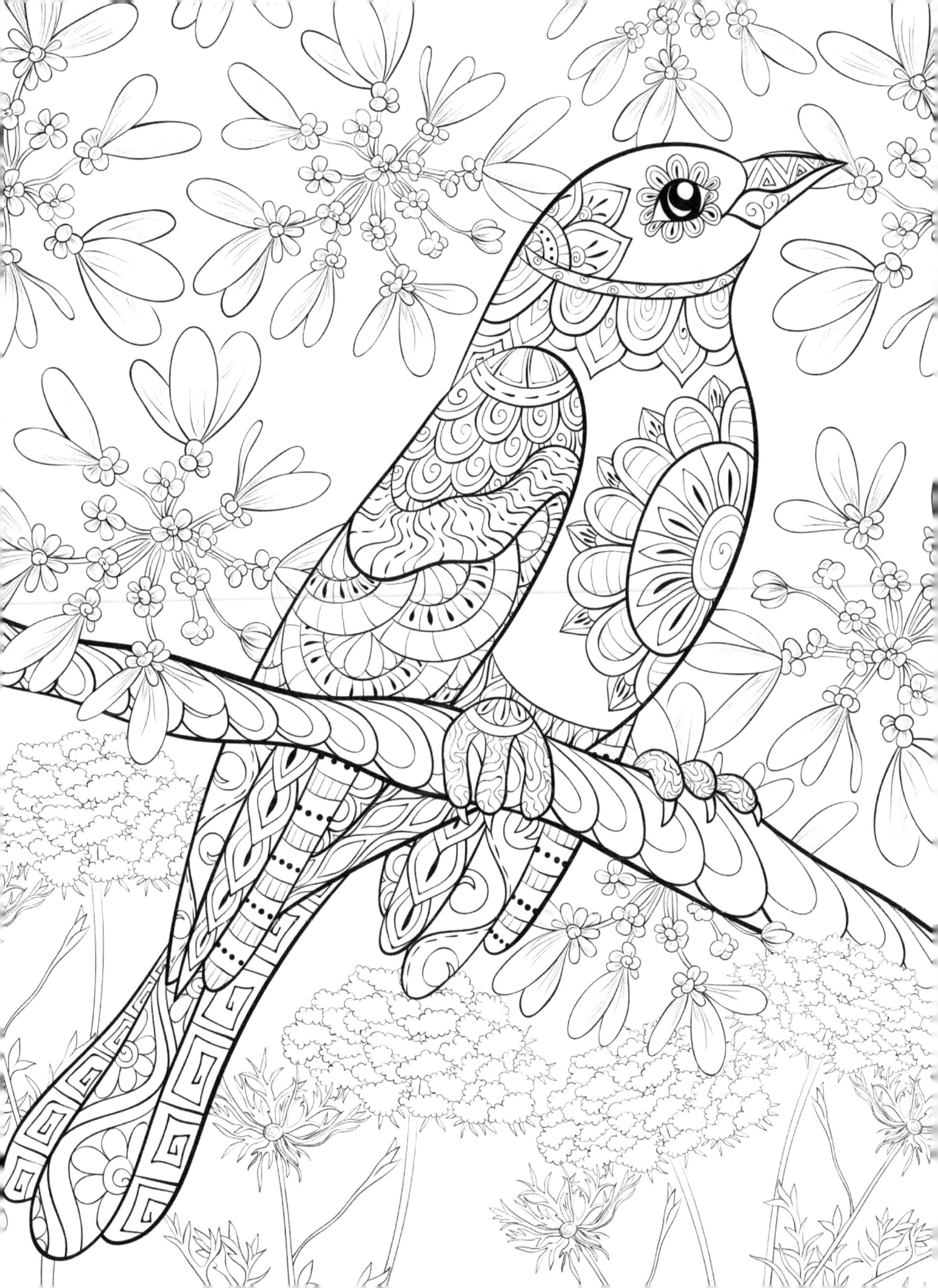

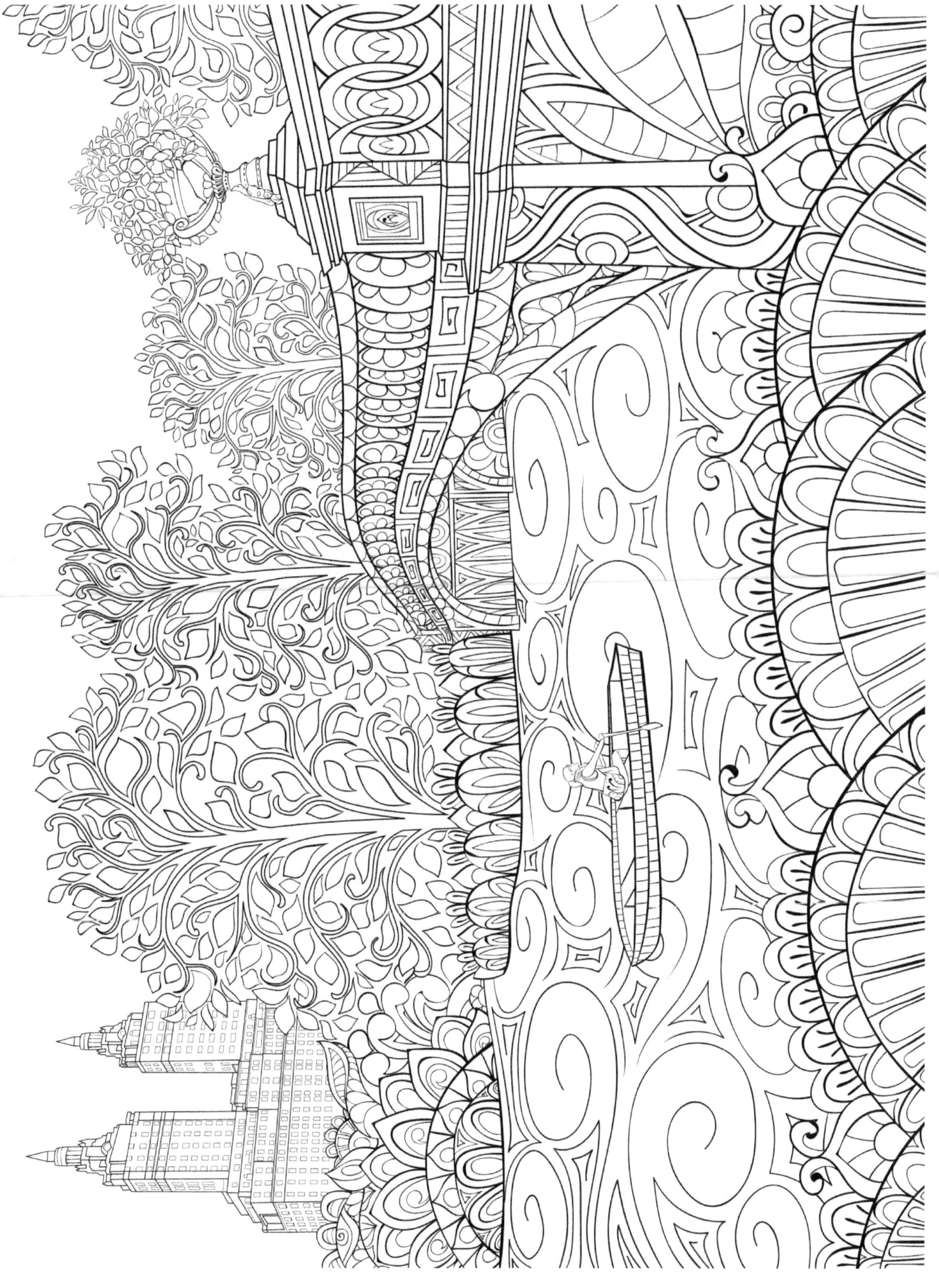

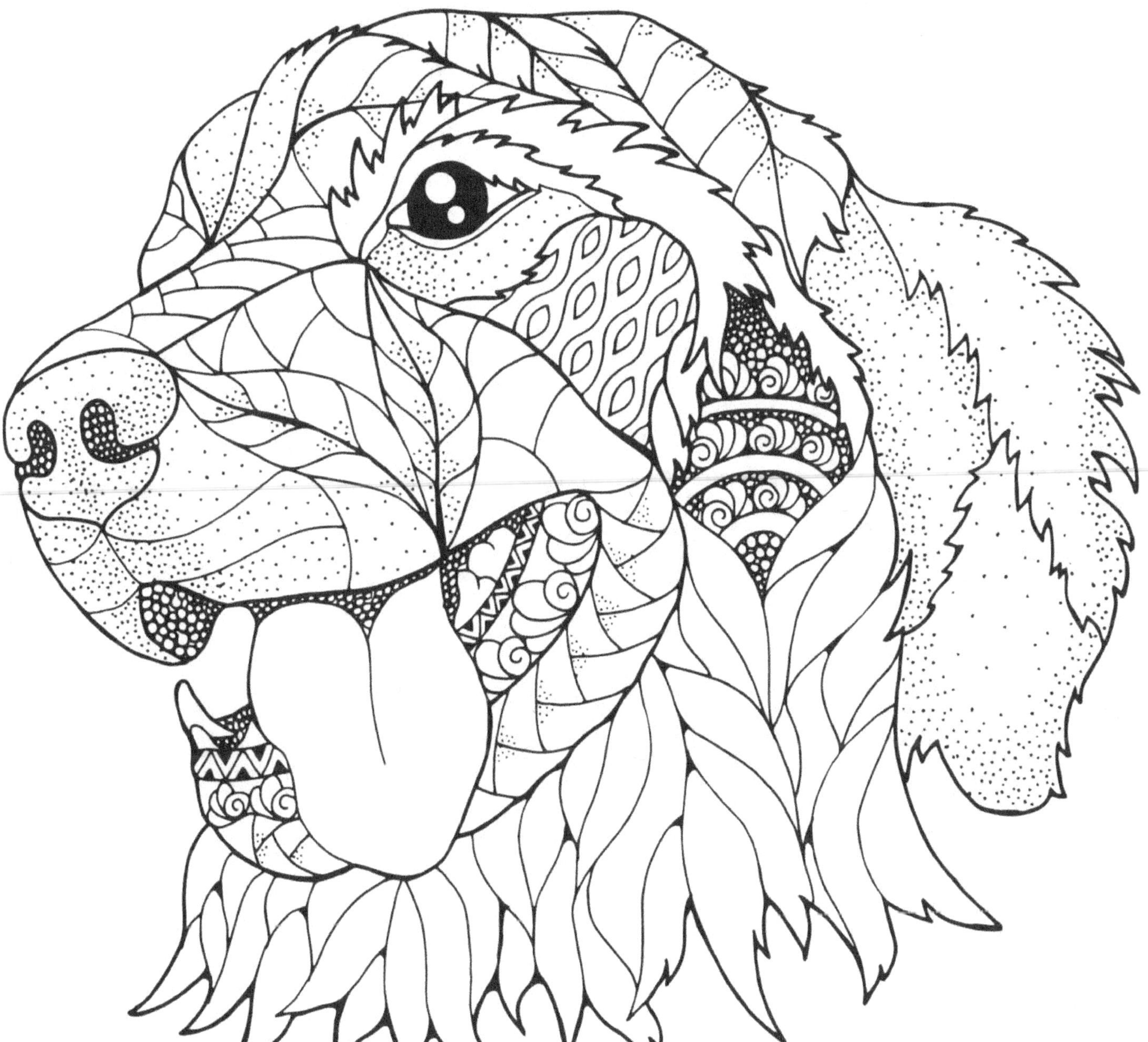

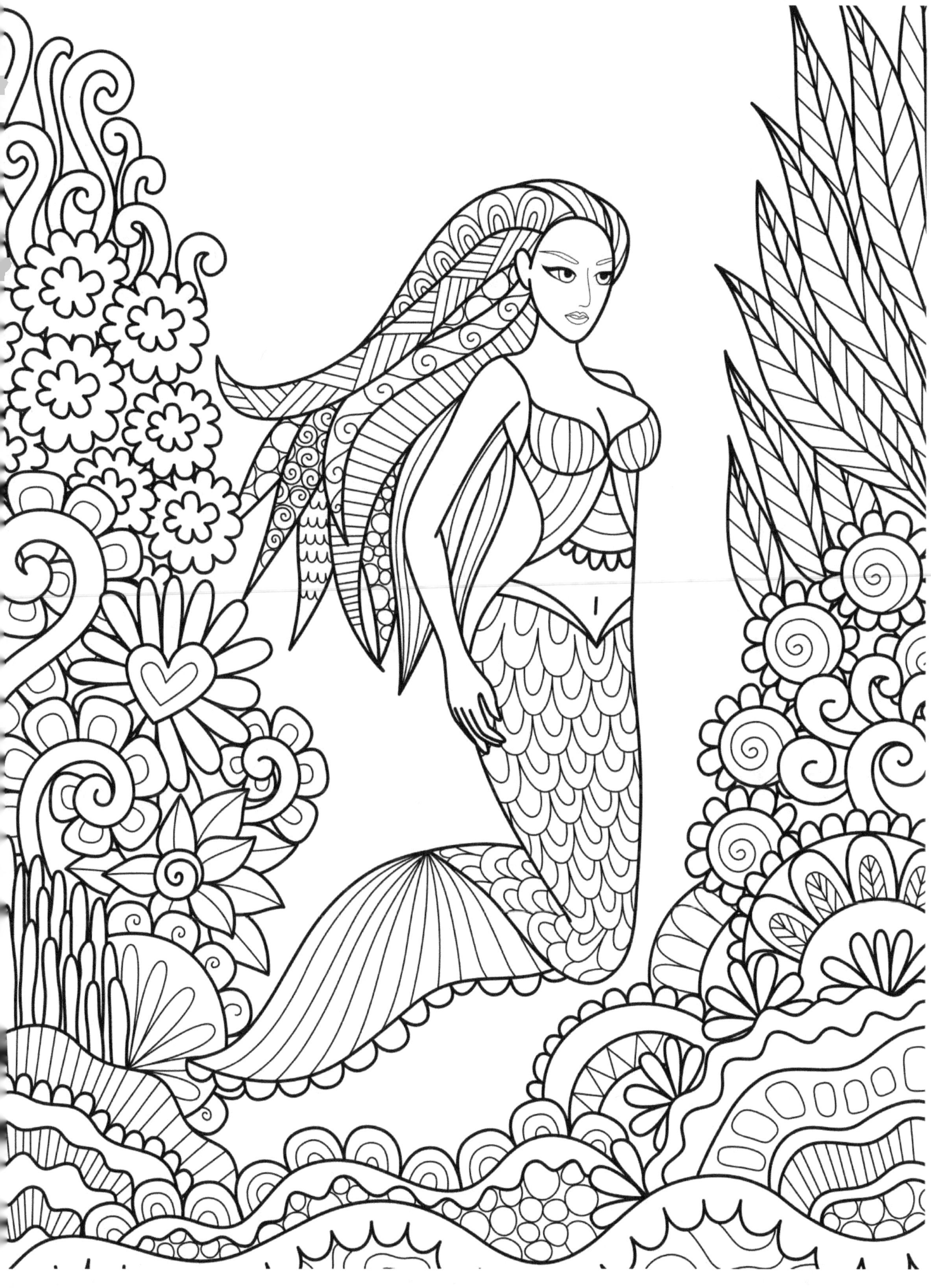

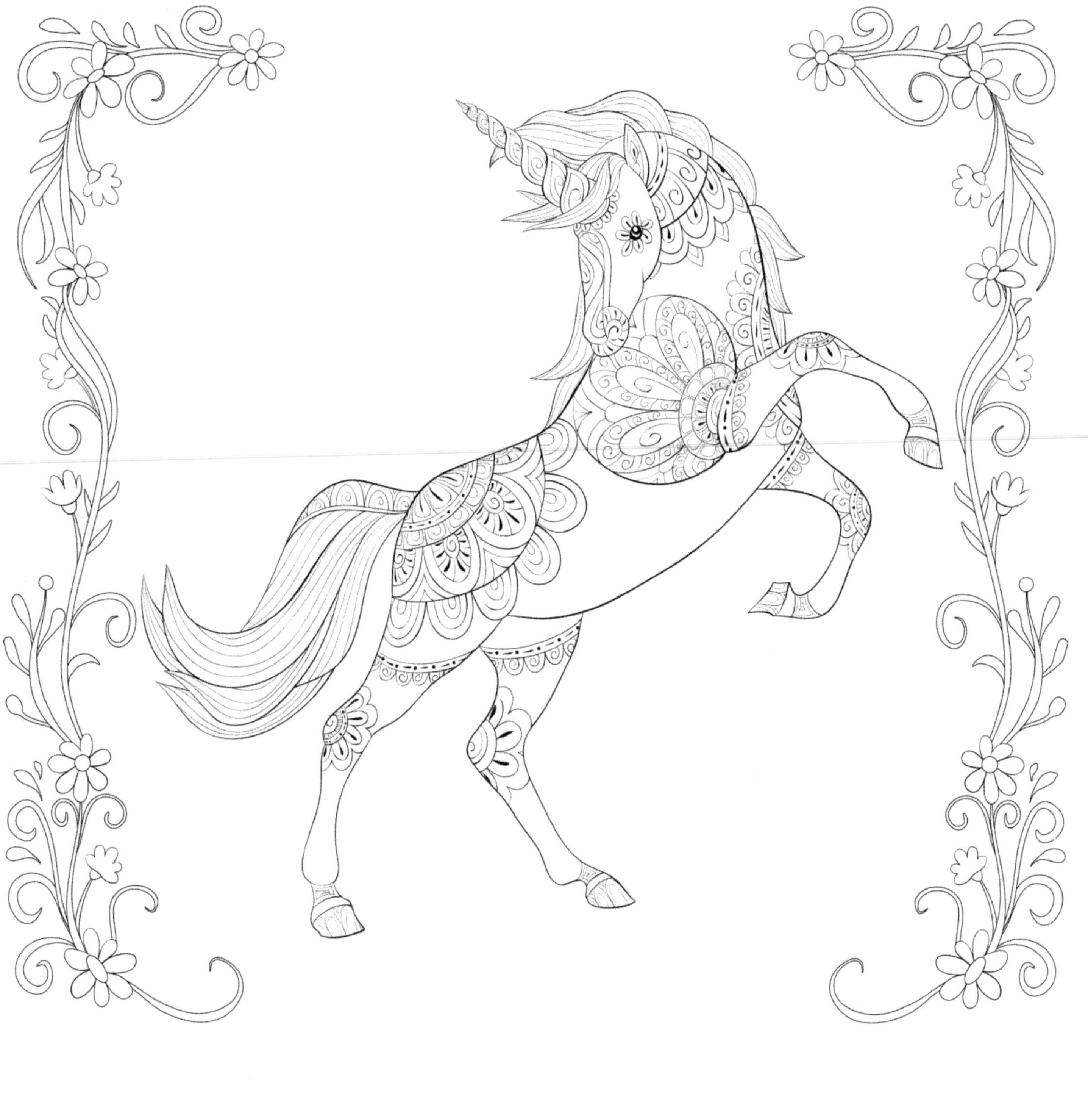

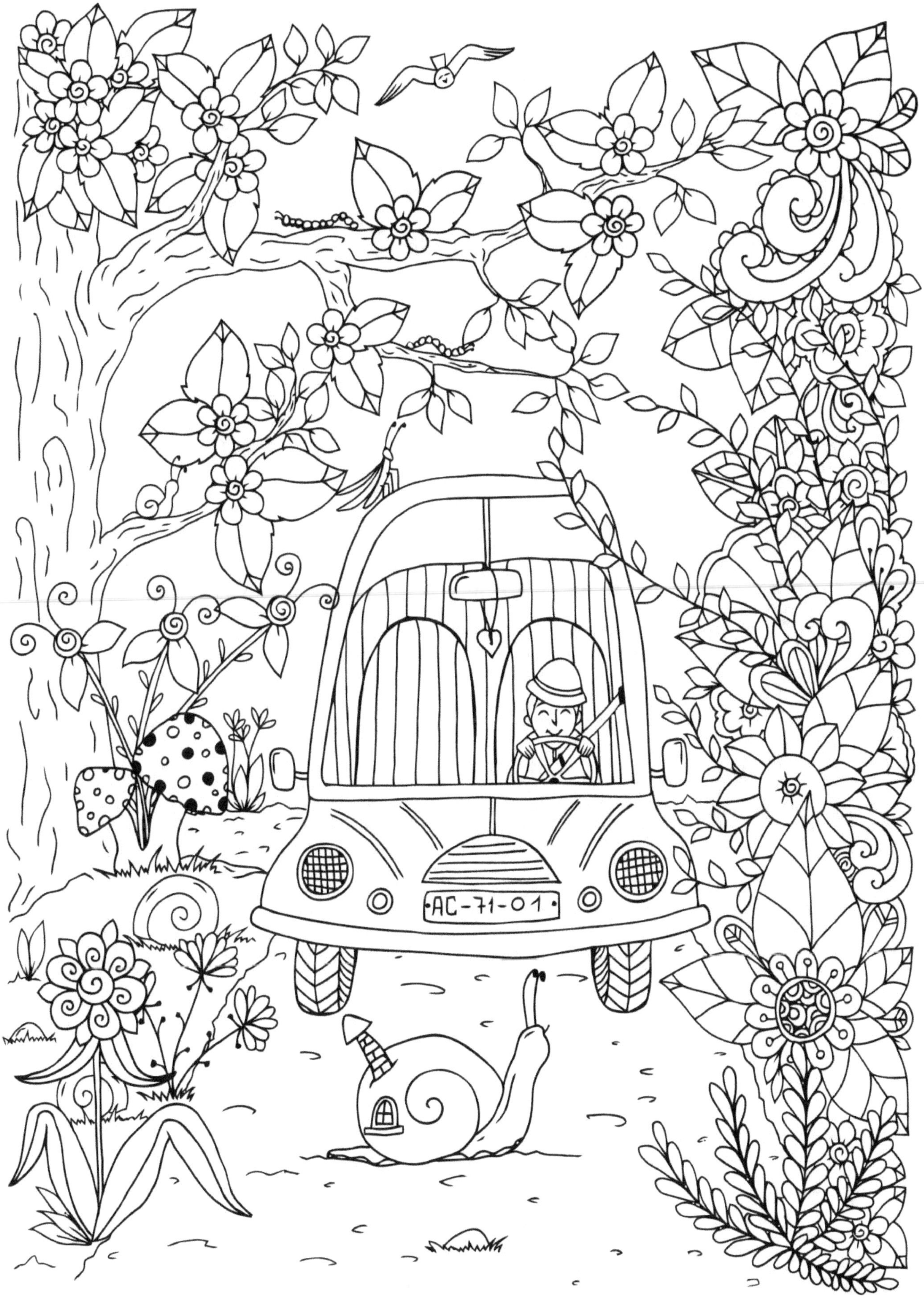
AC-71-01

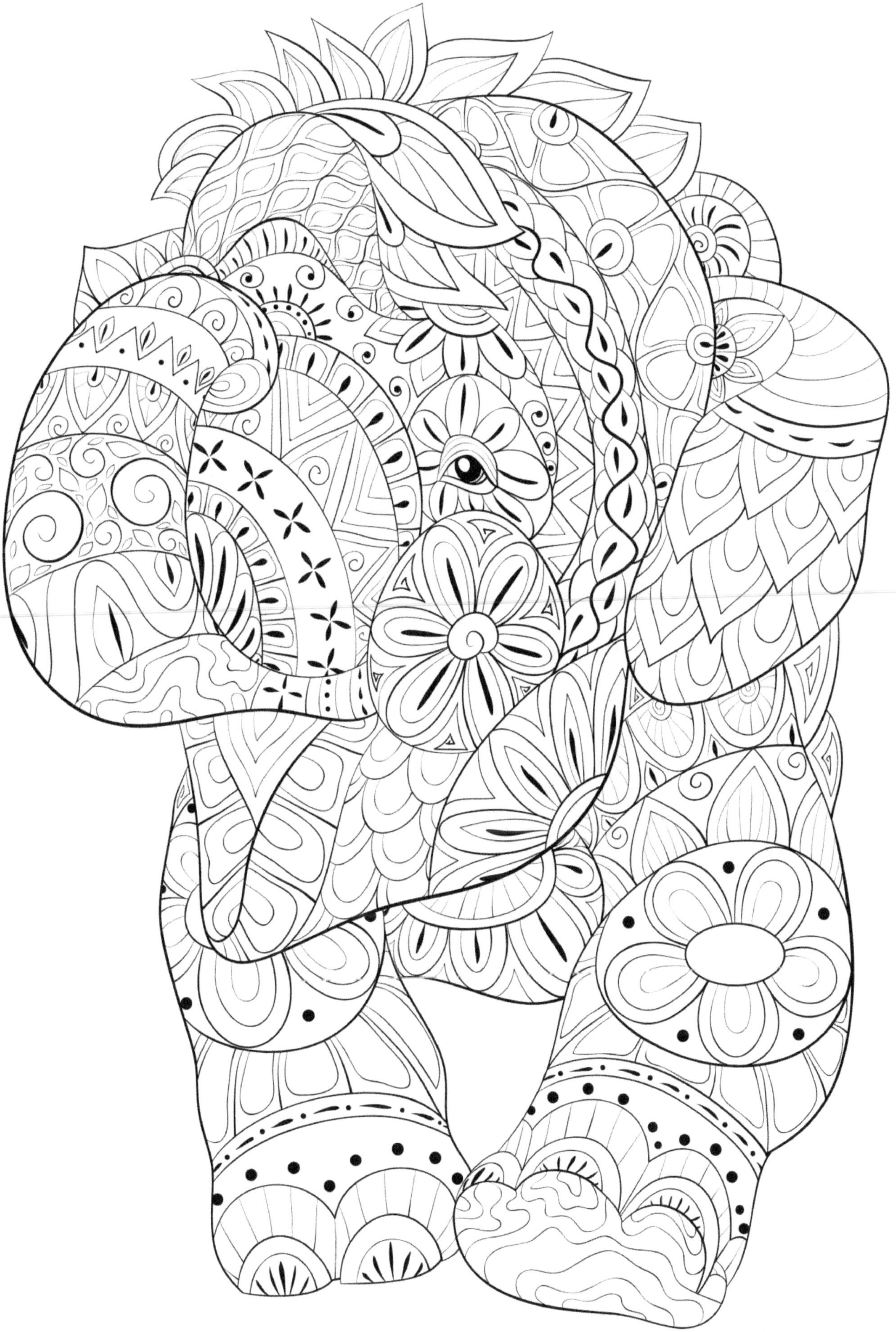

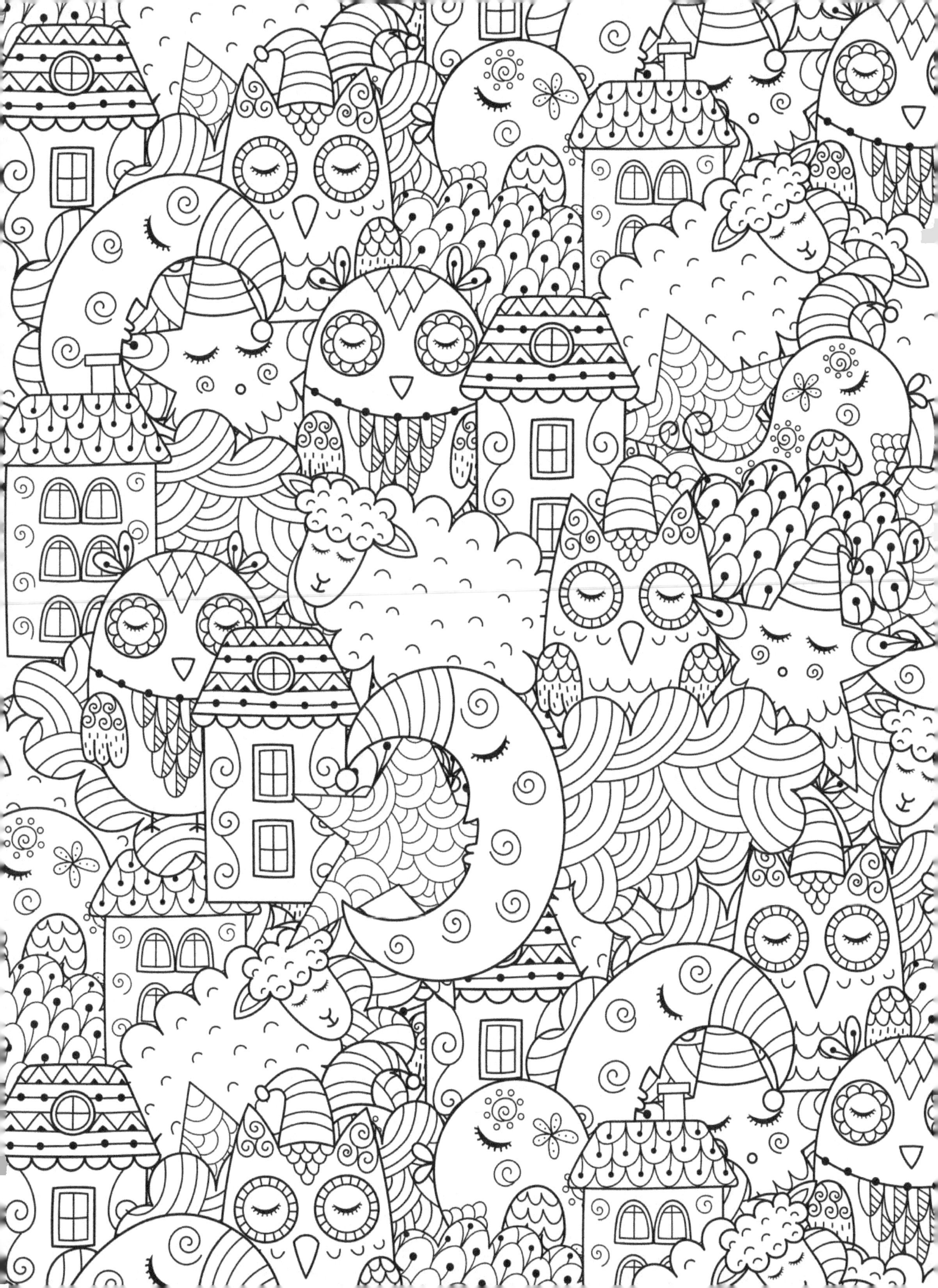

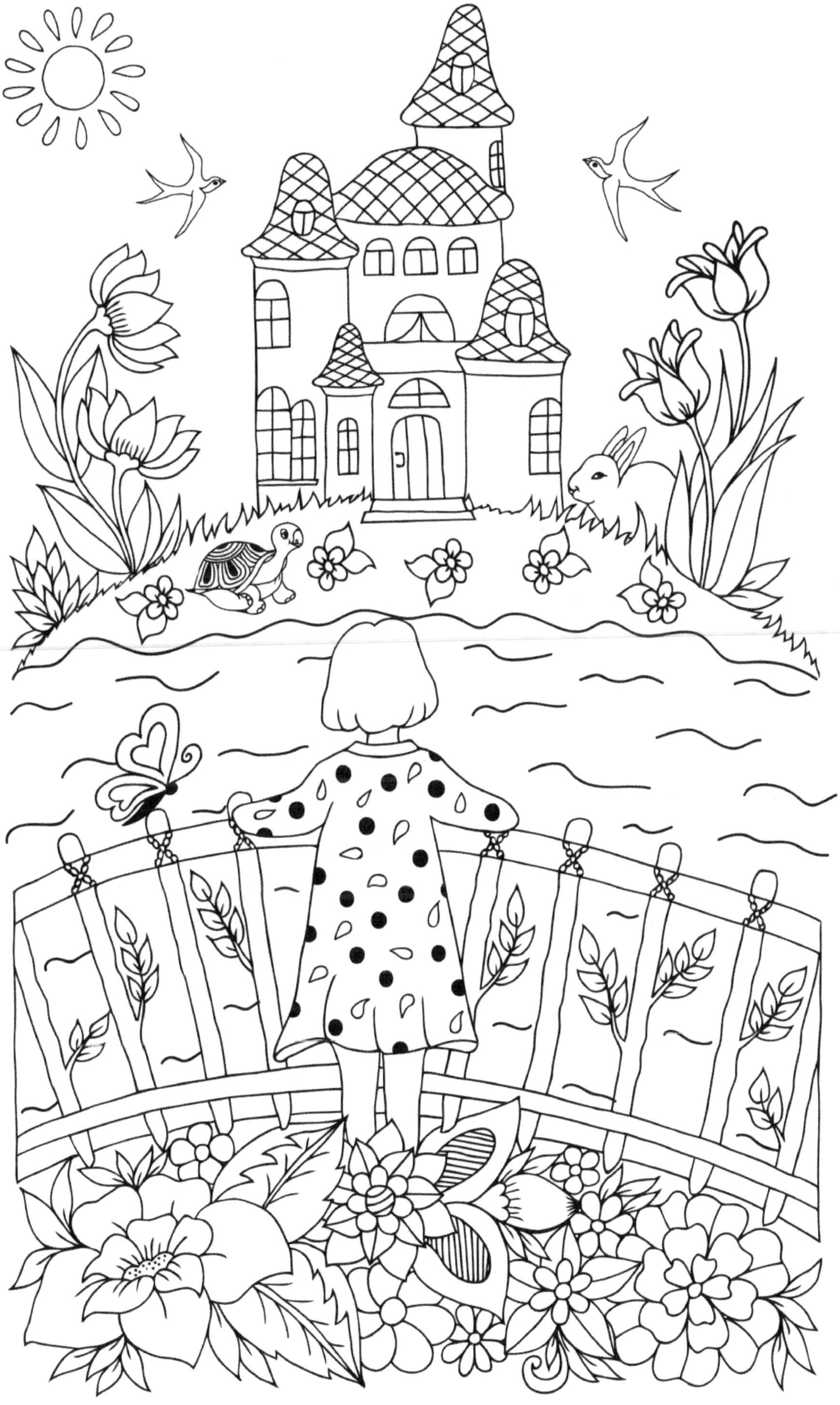

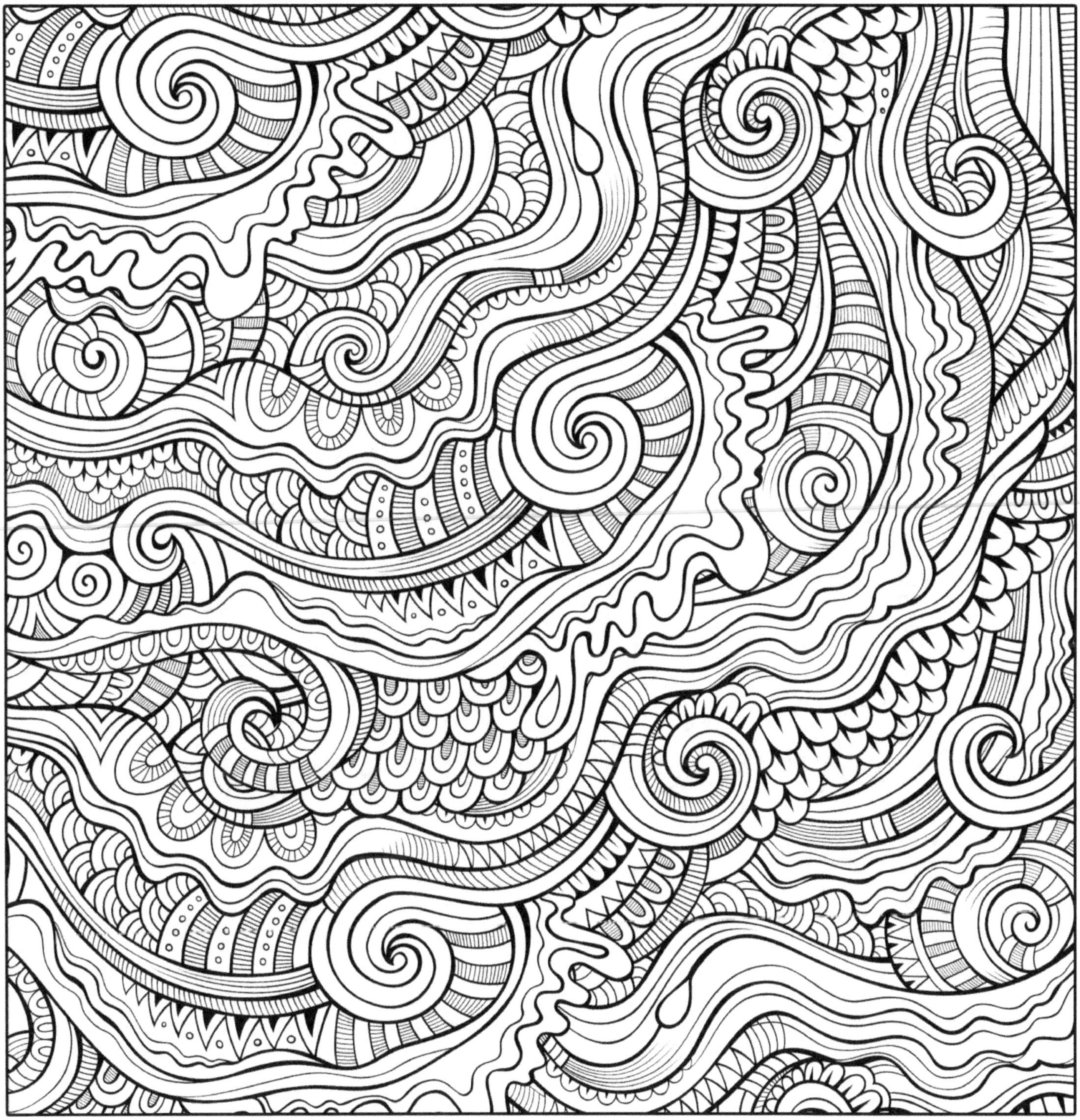

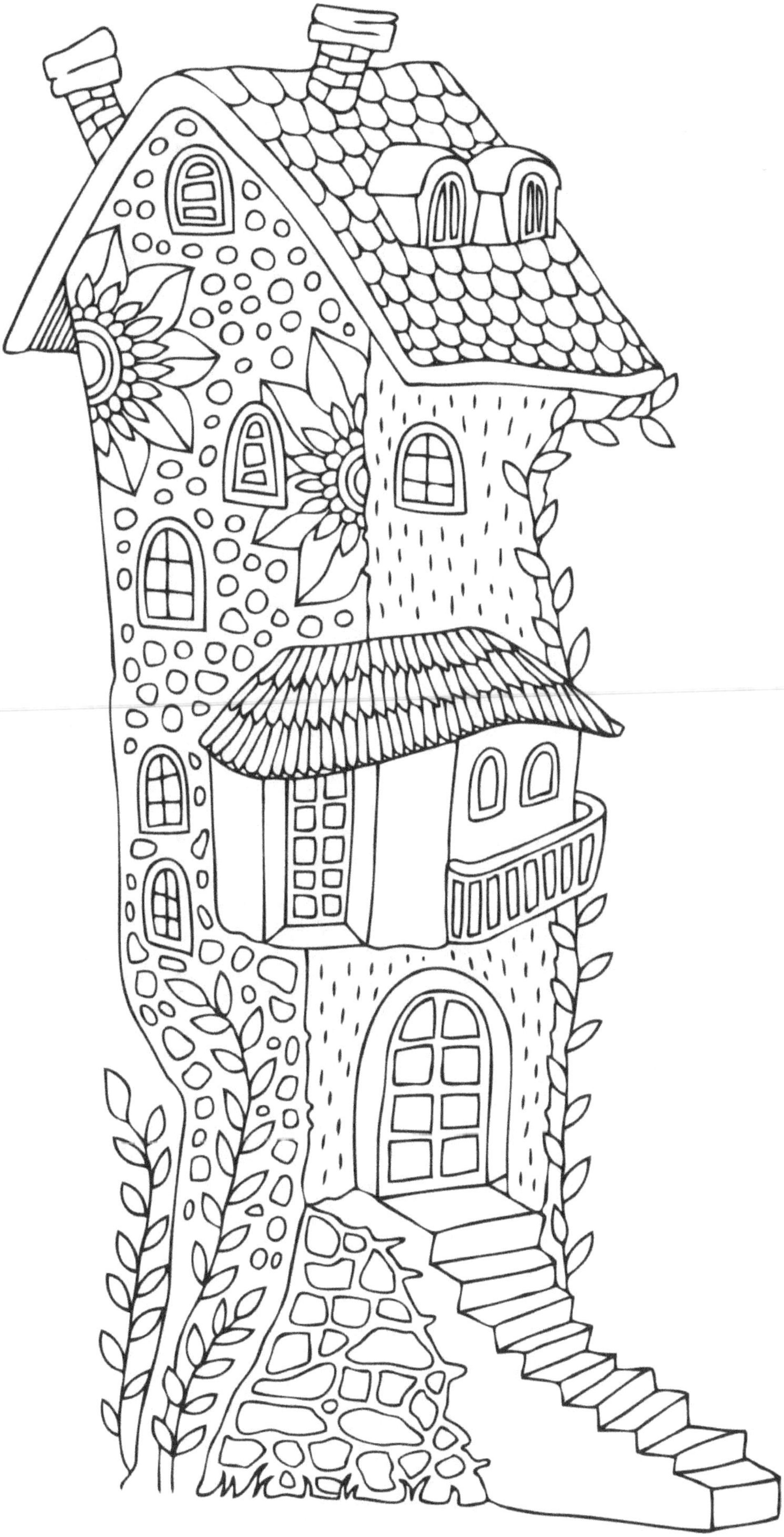

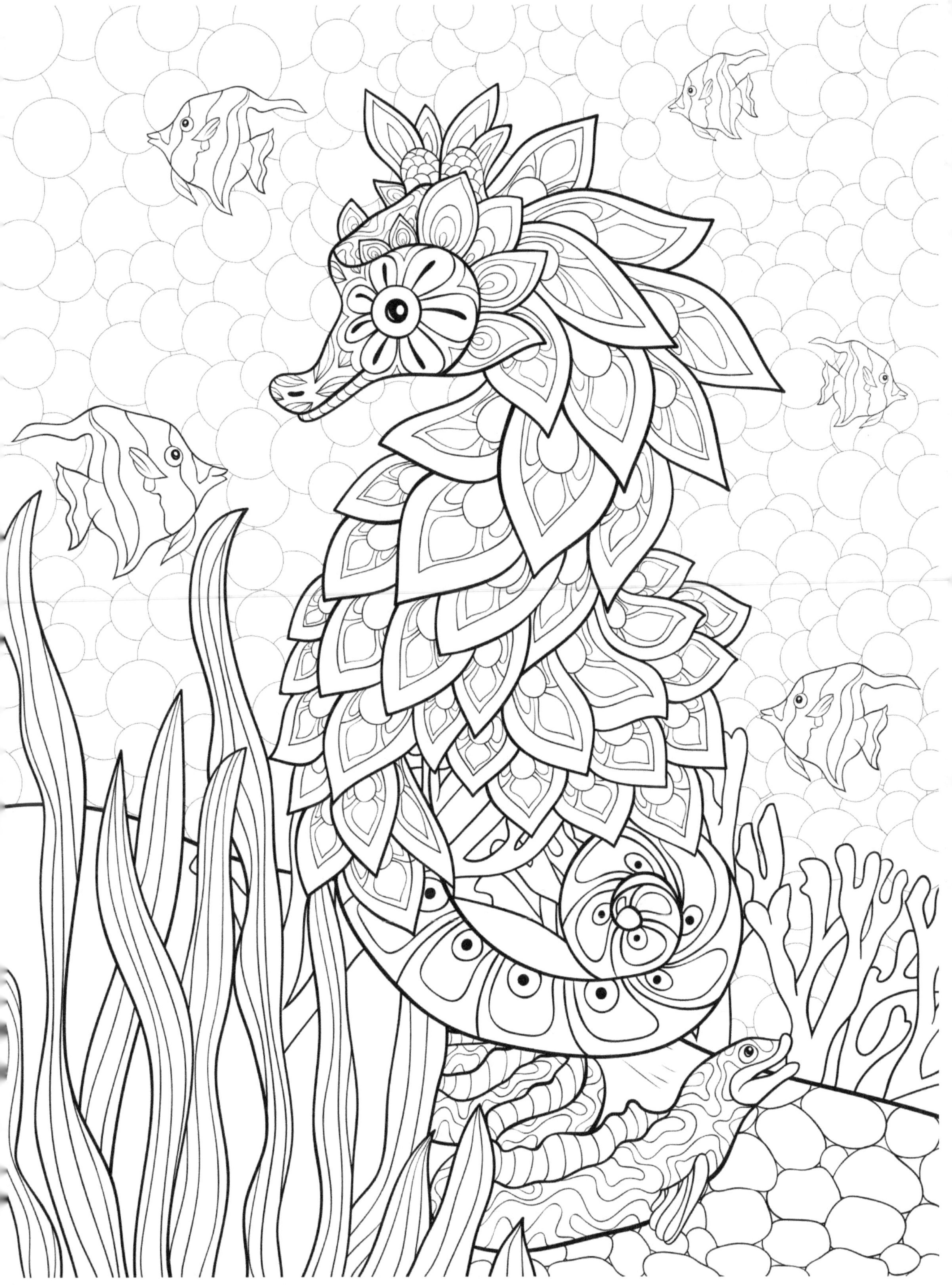

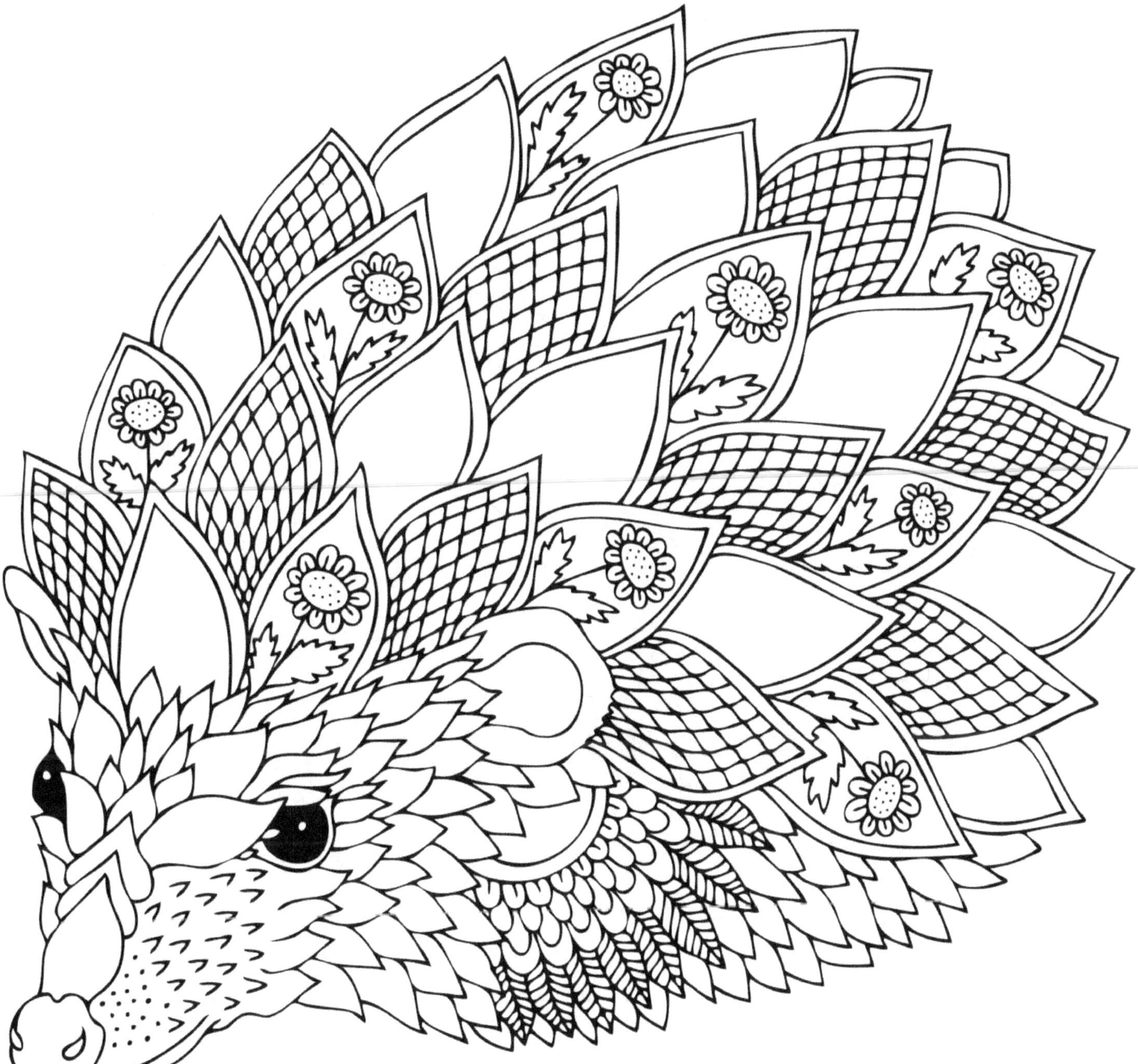

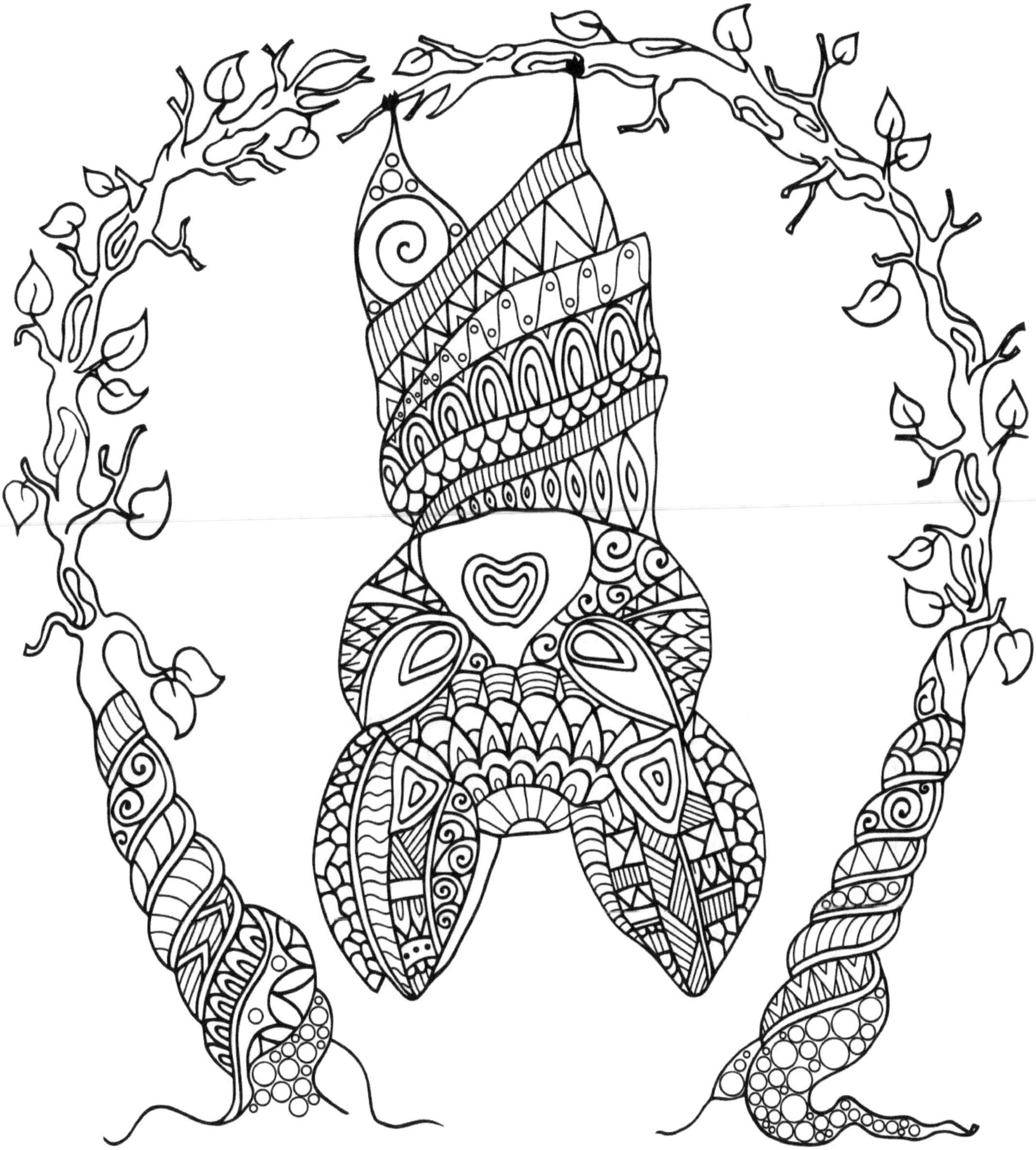

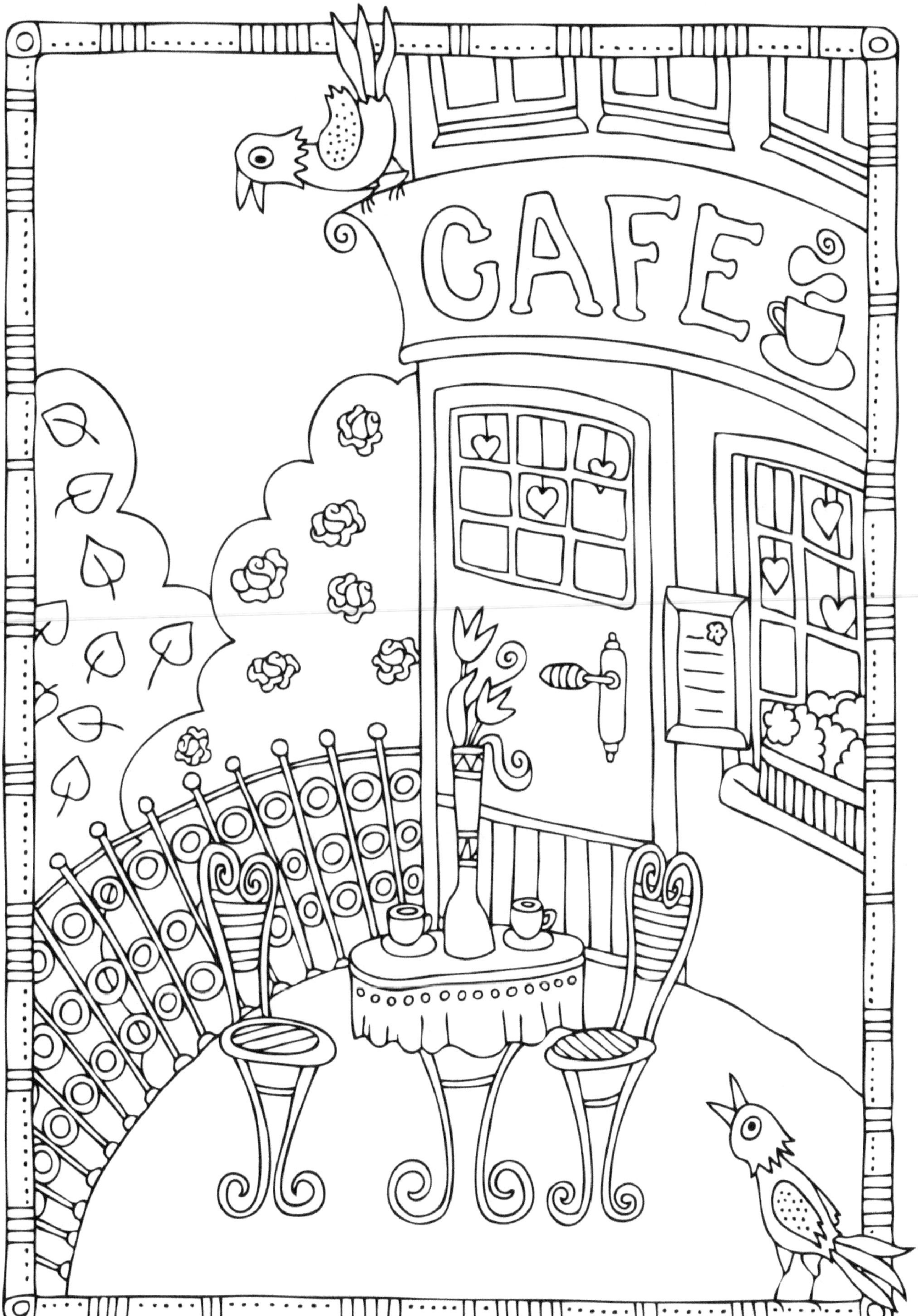
CAFE

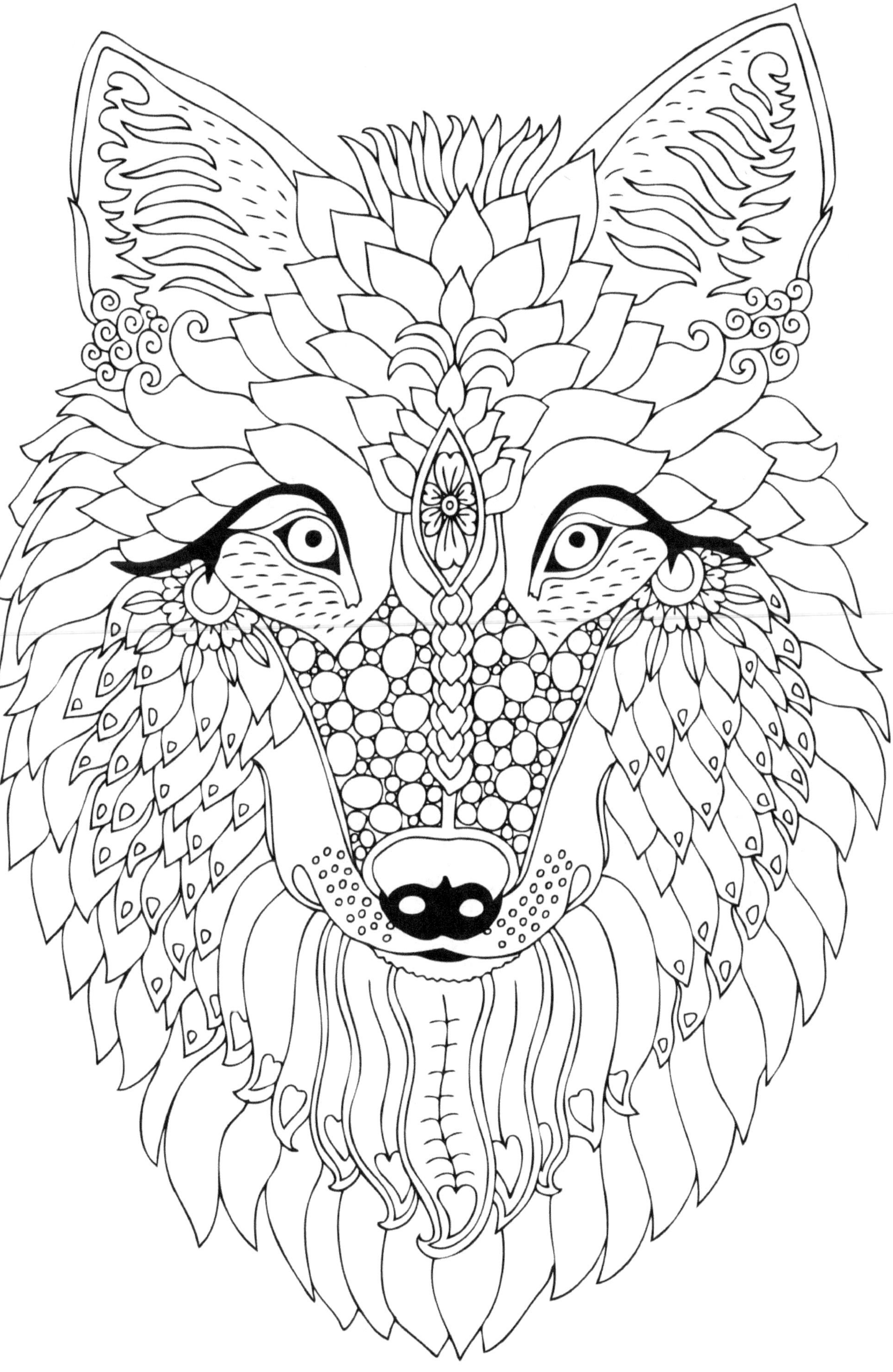

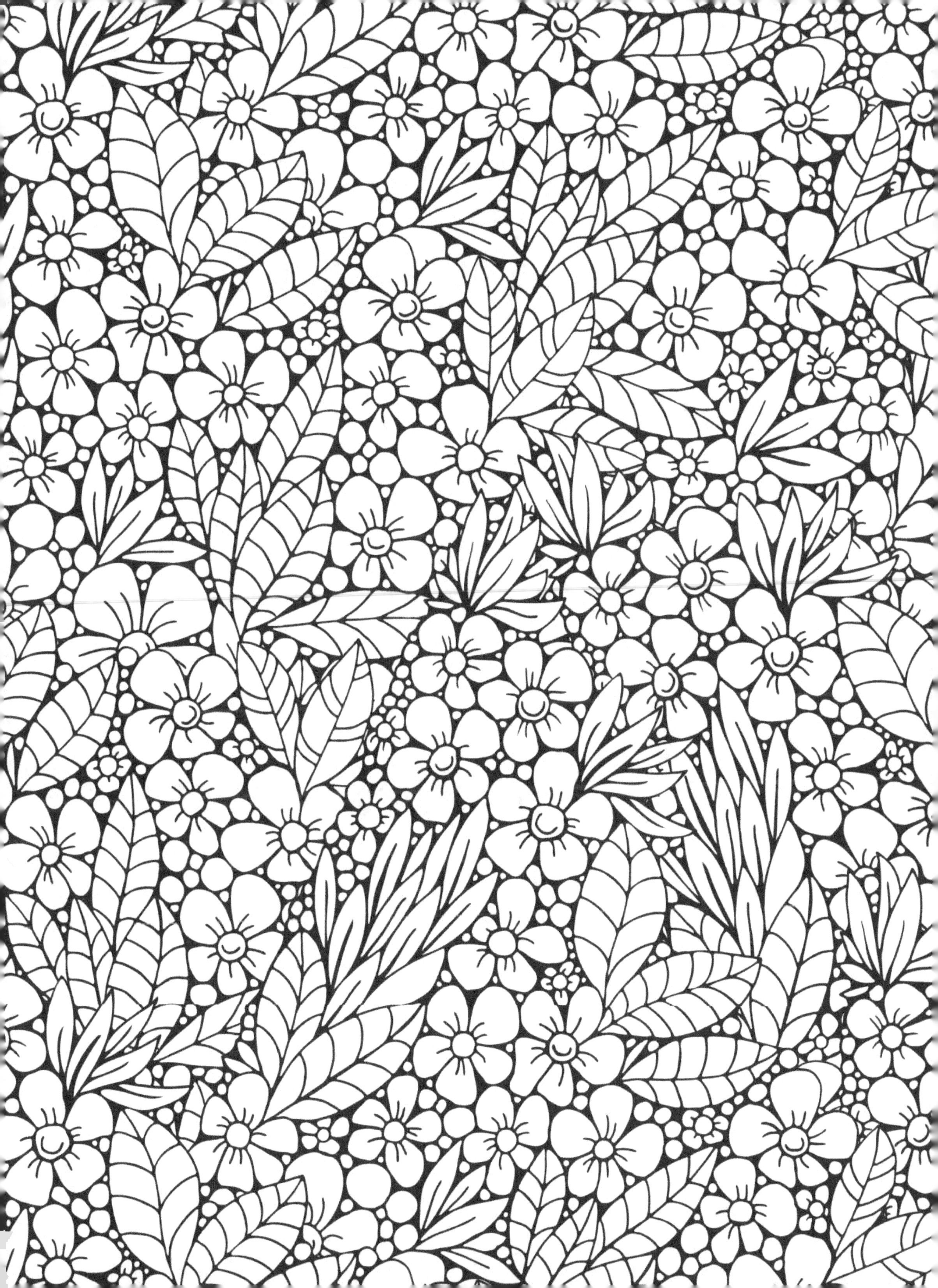

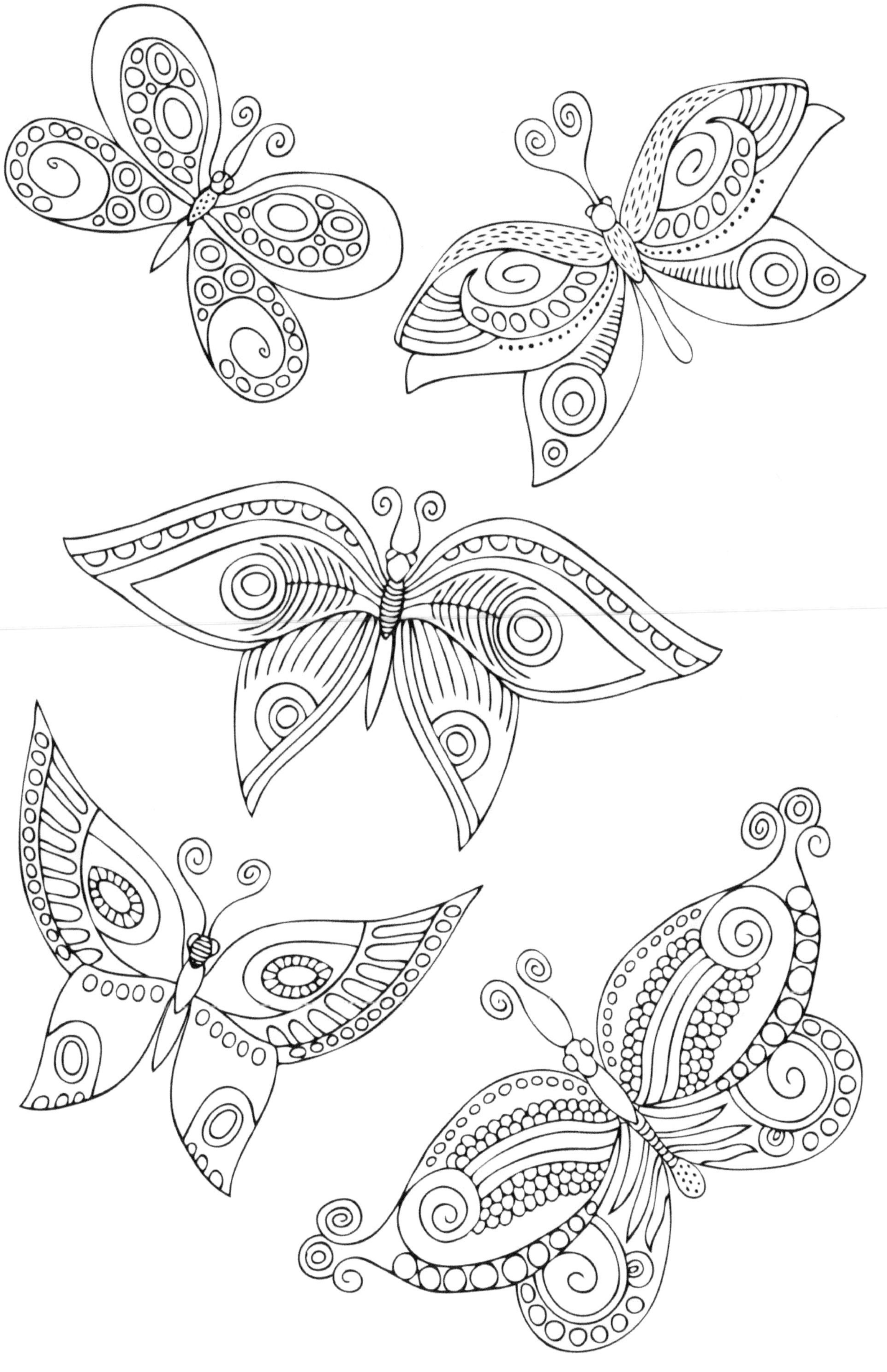

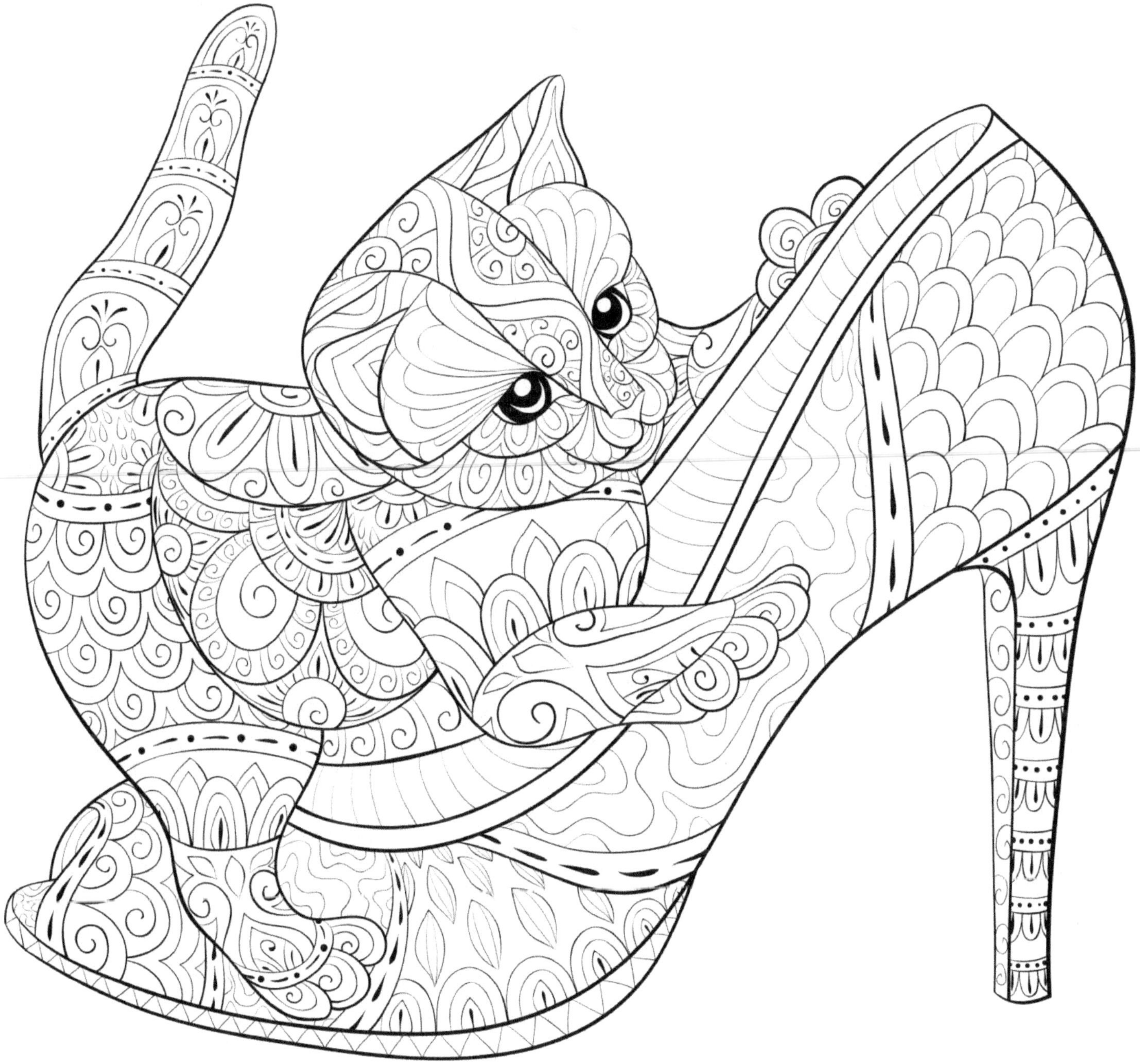

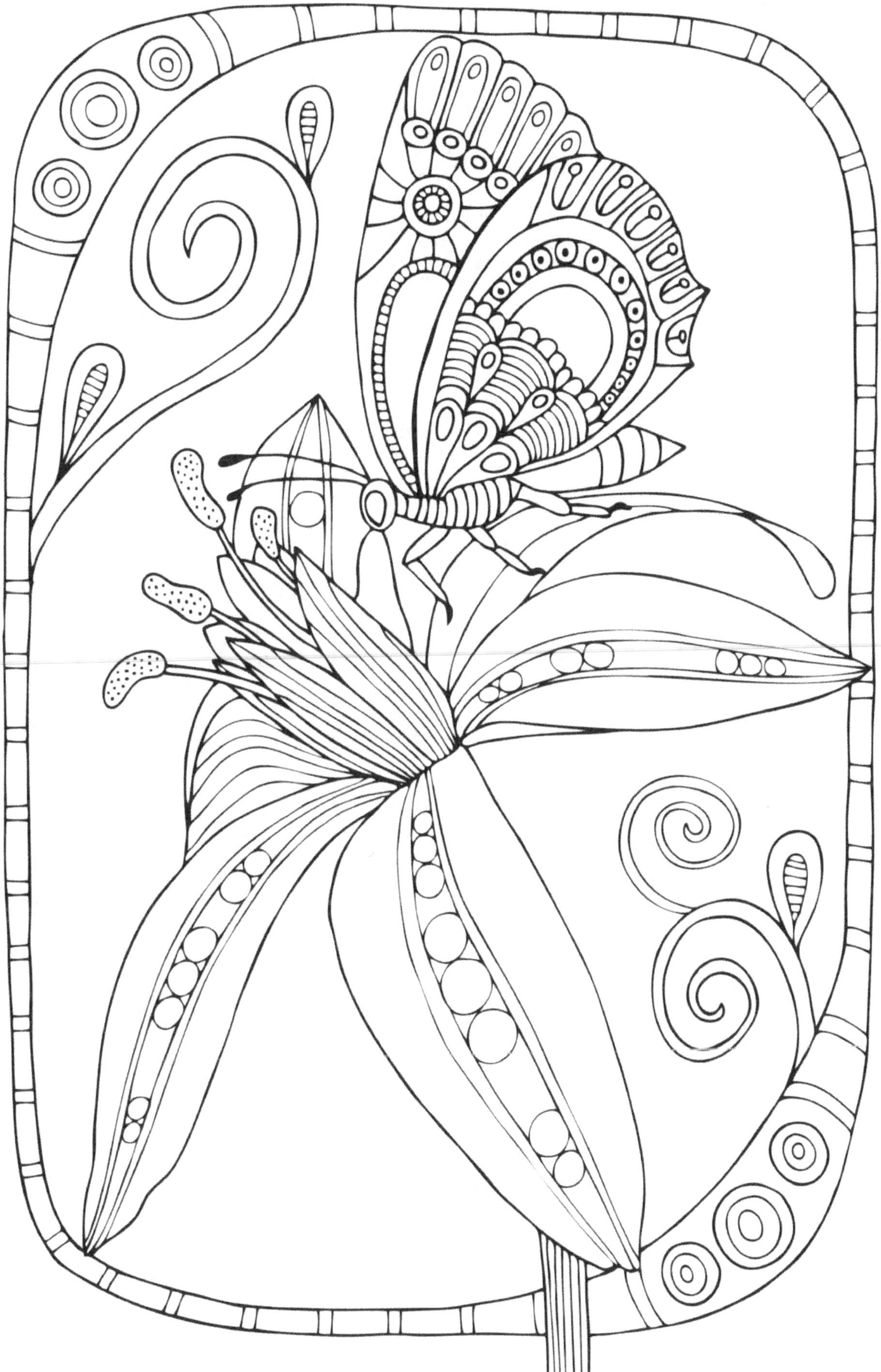

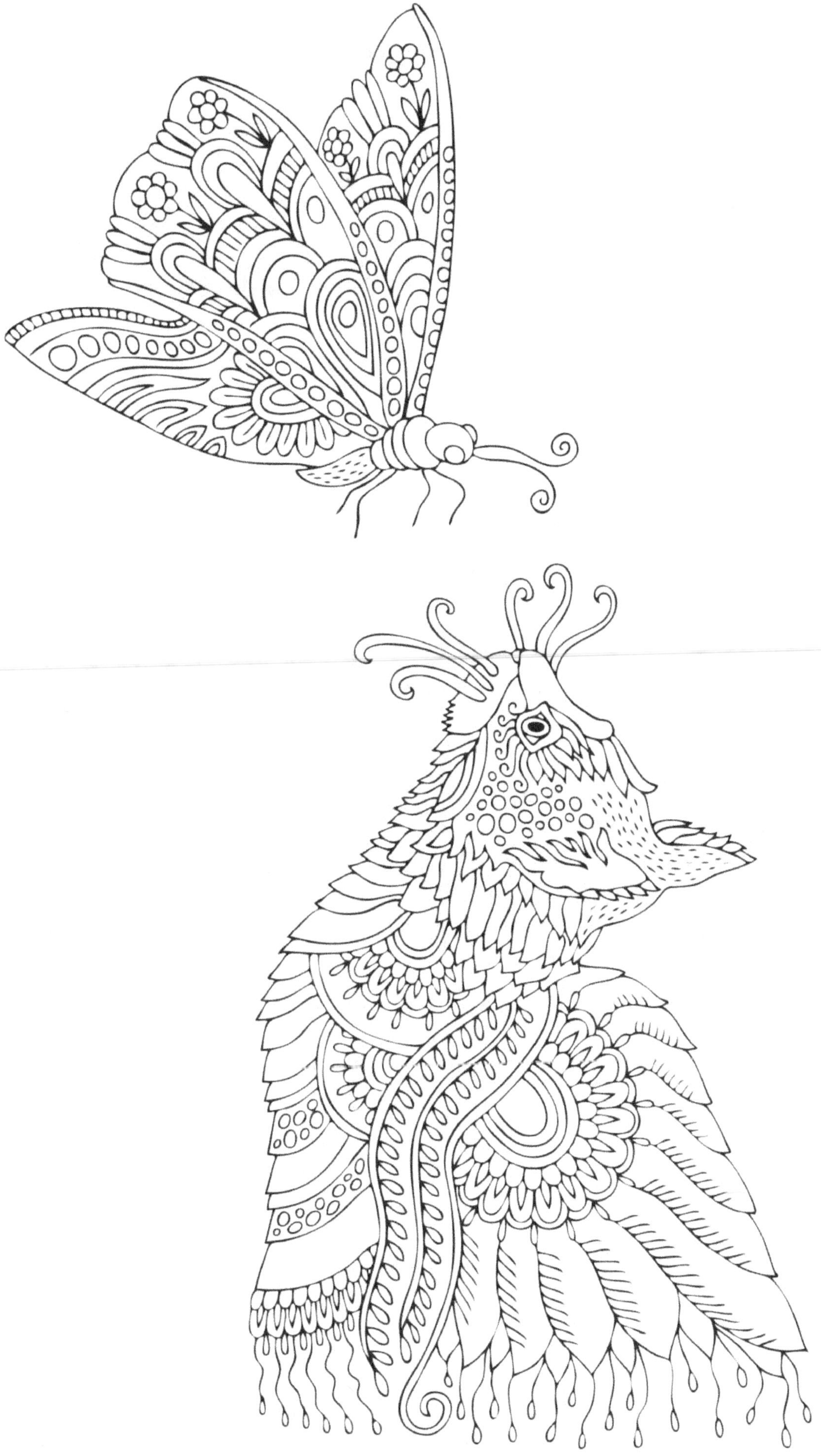

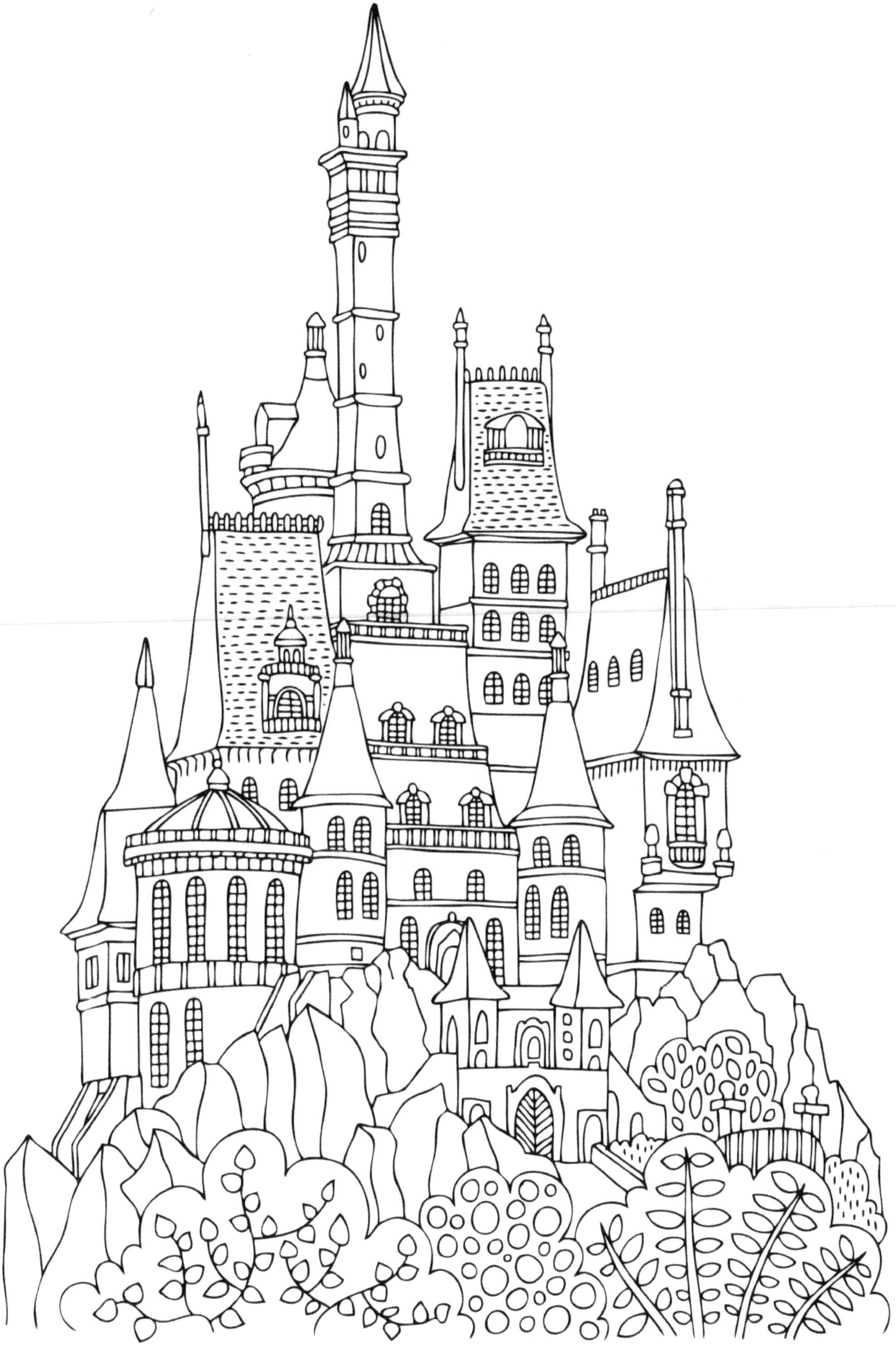

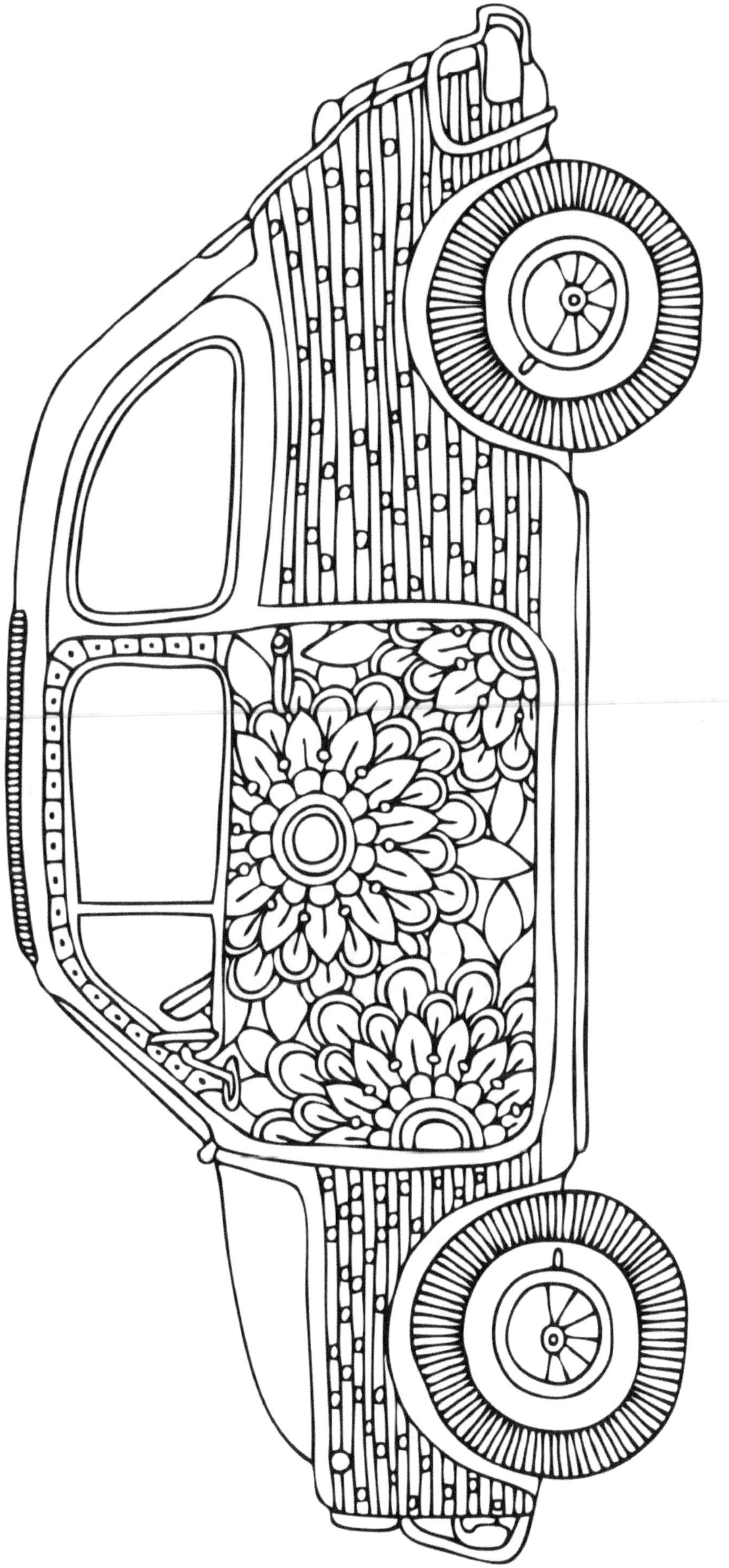

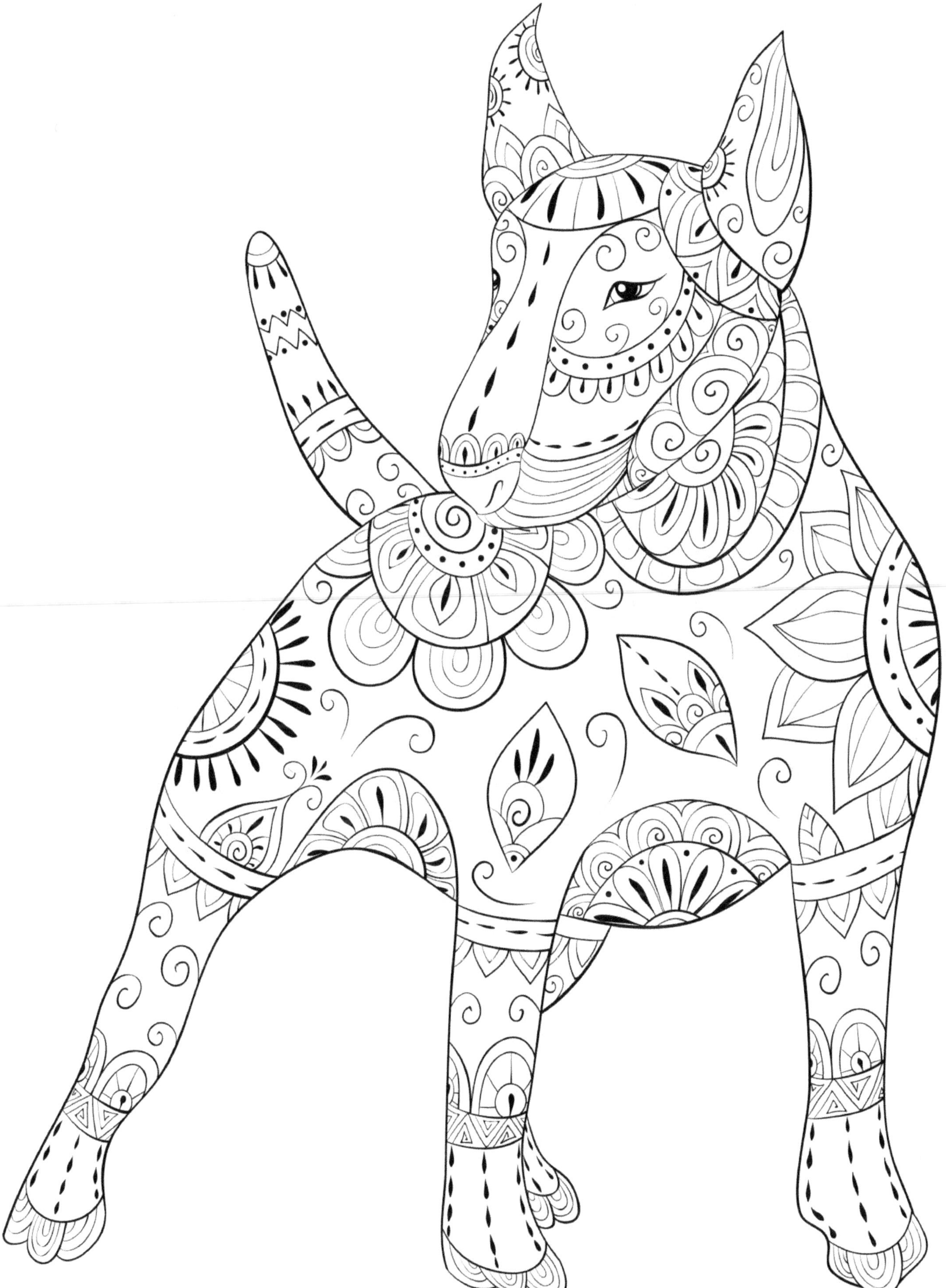

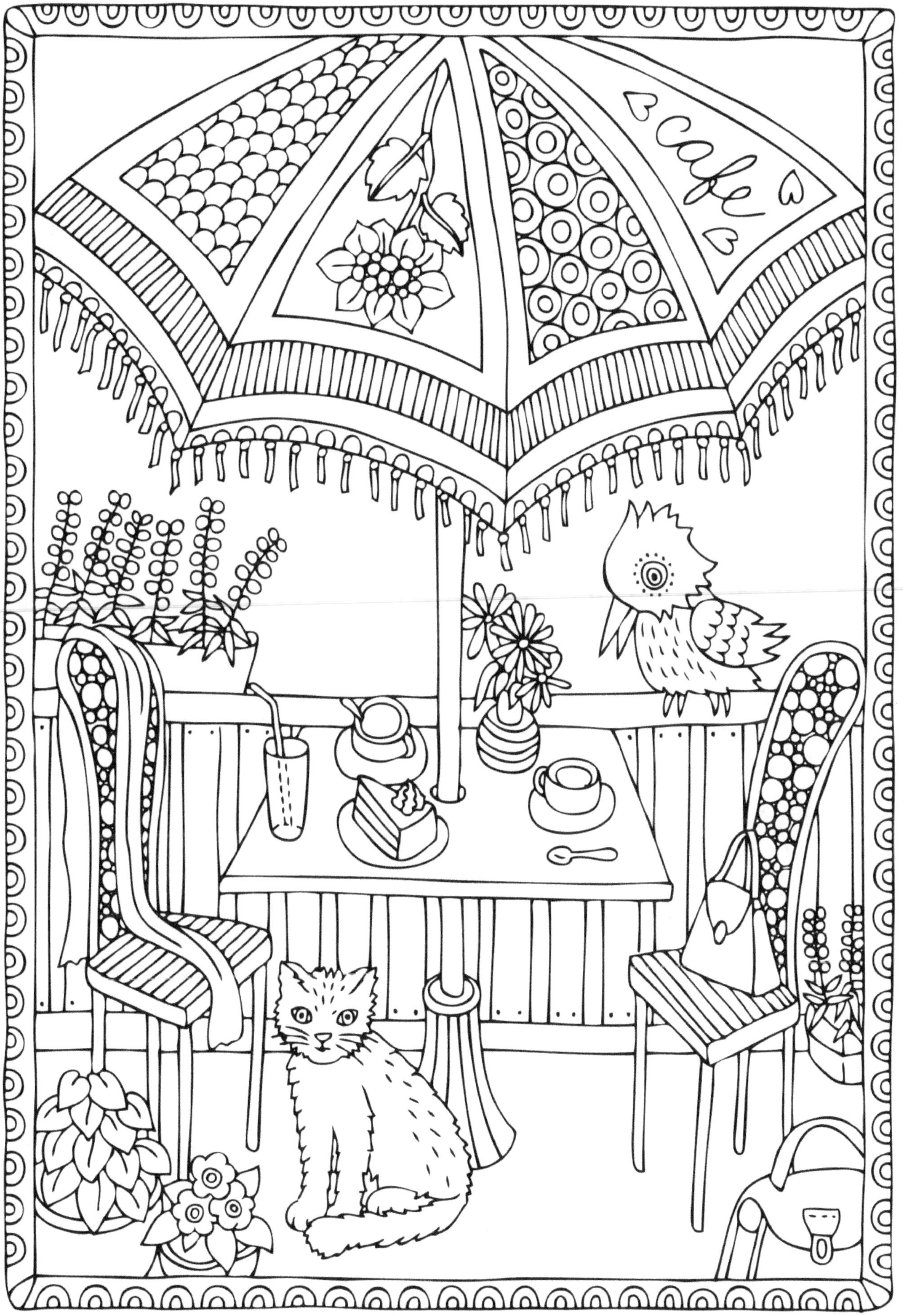
cafe

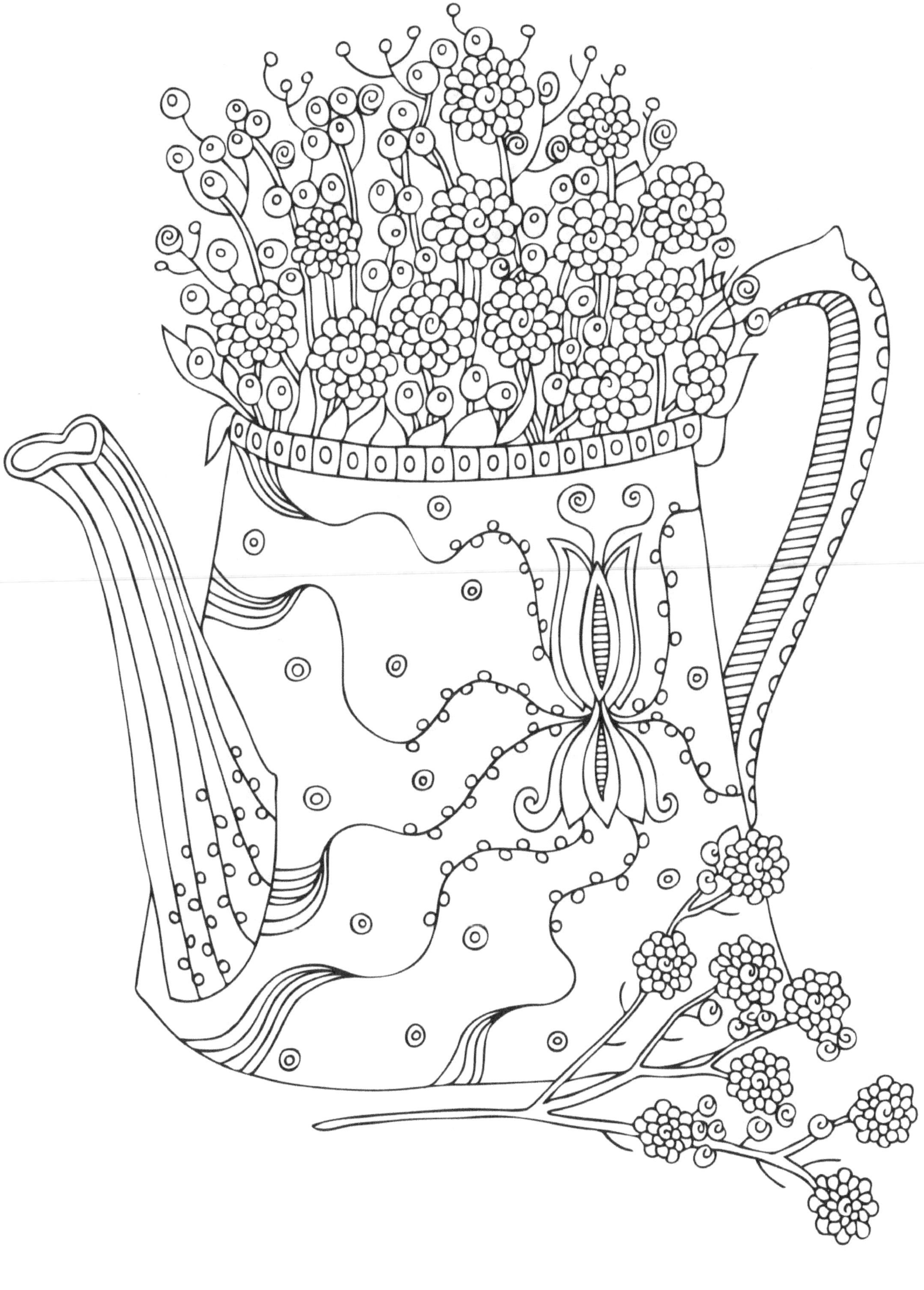

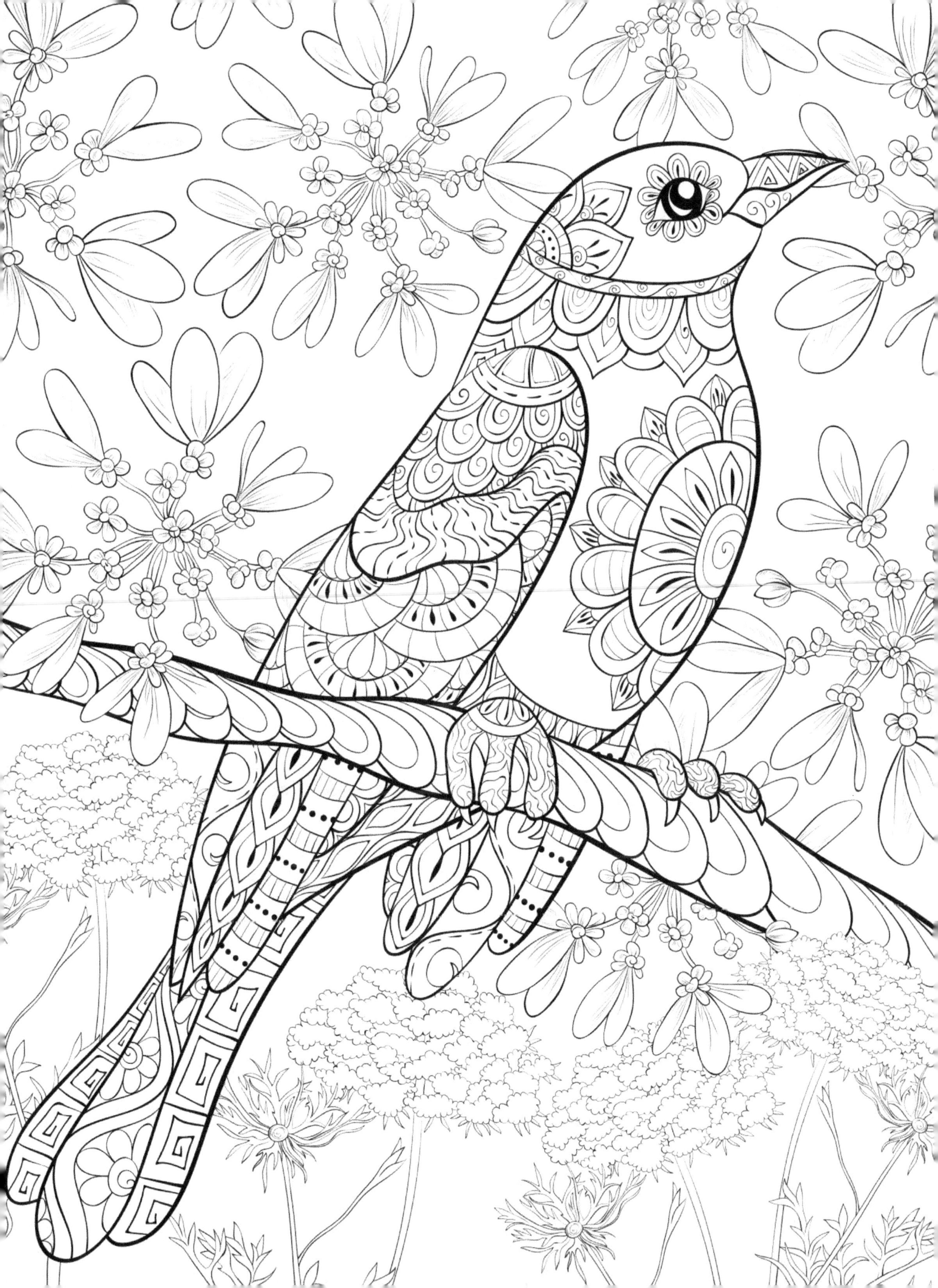

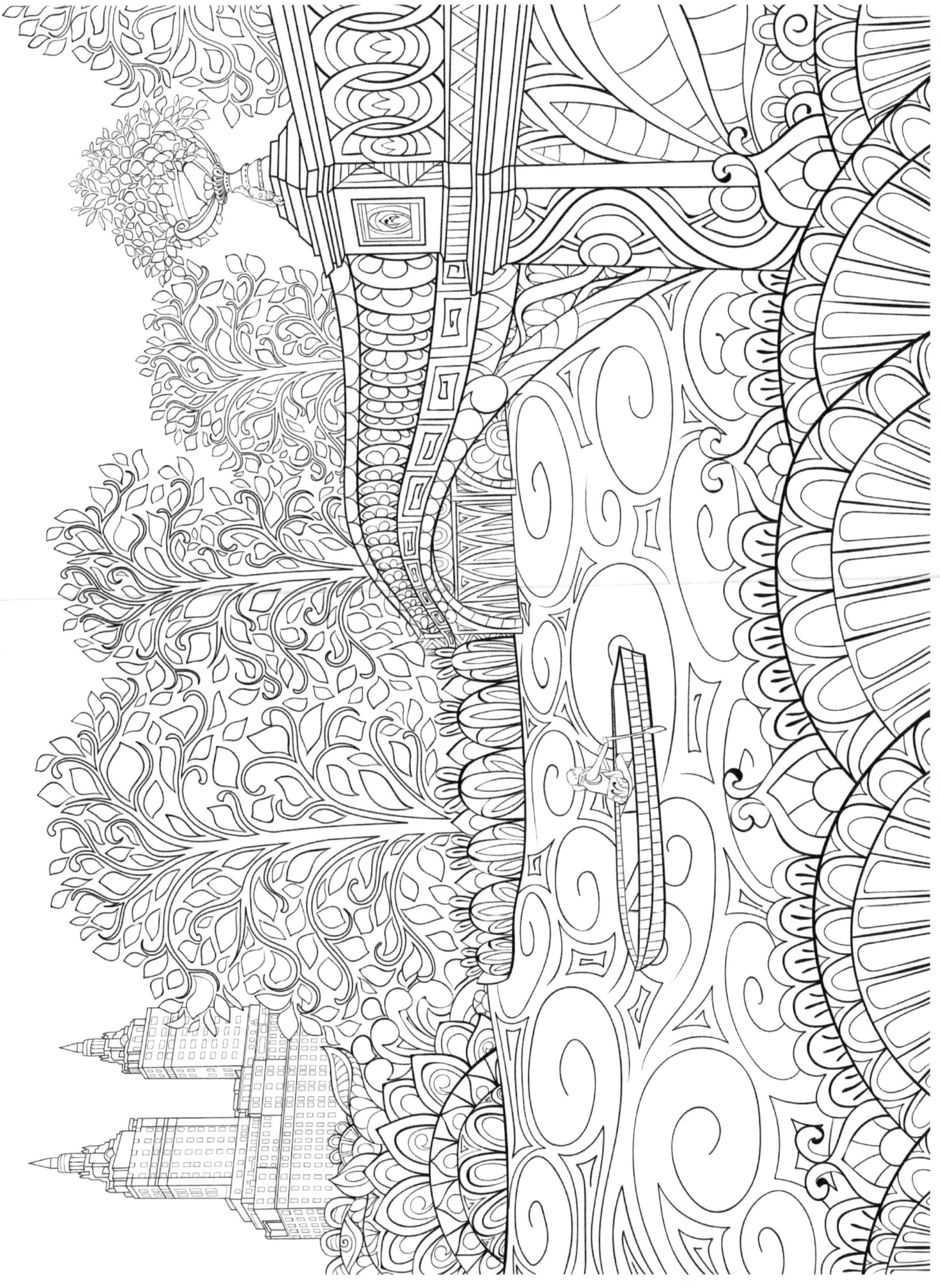

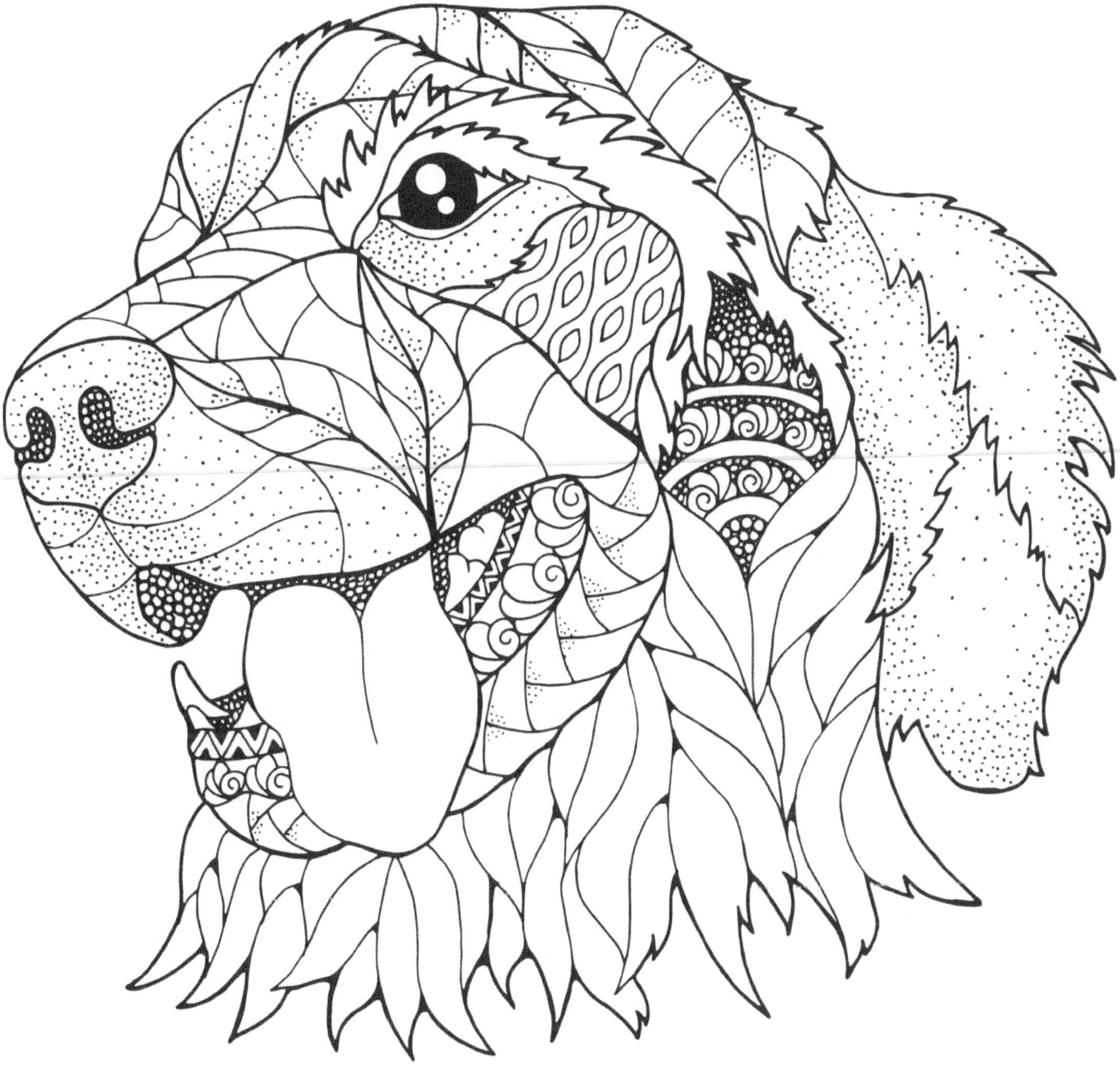

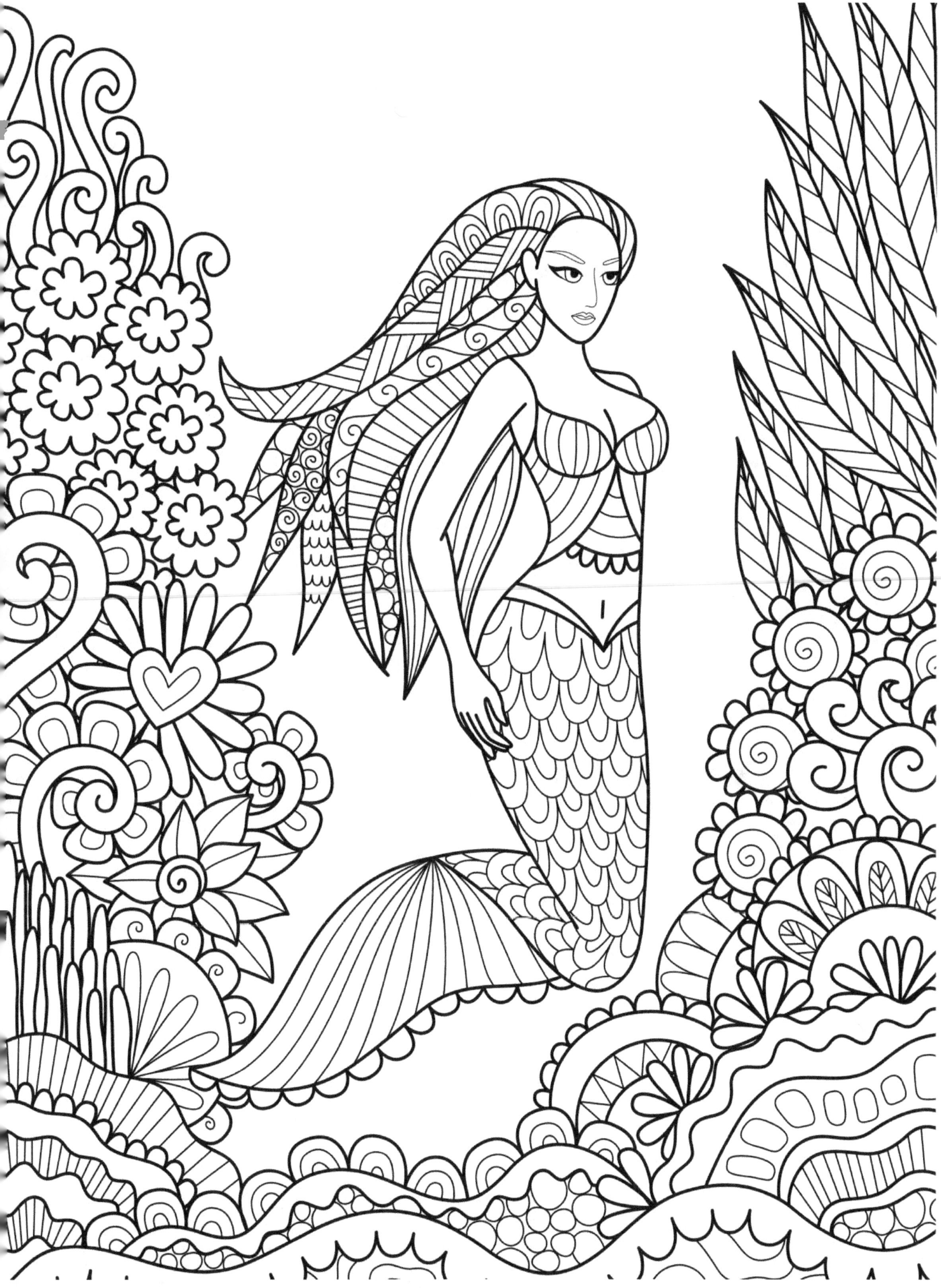

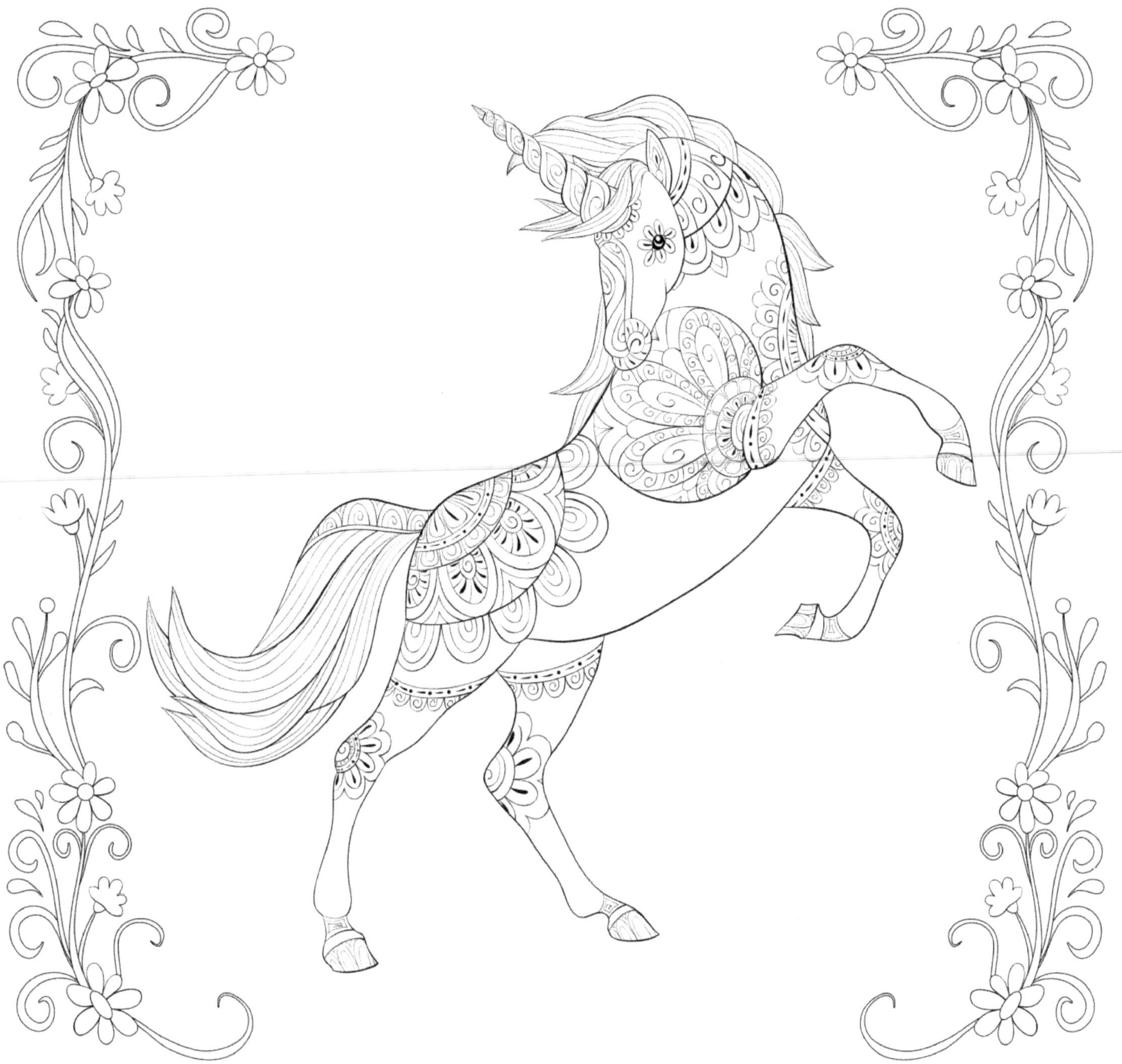

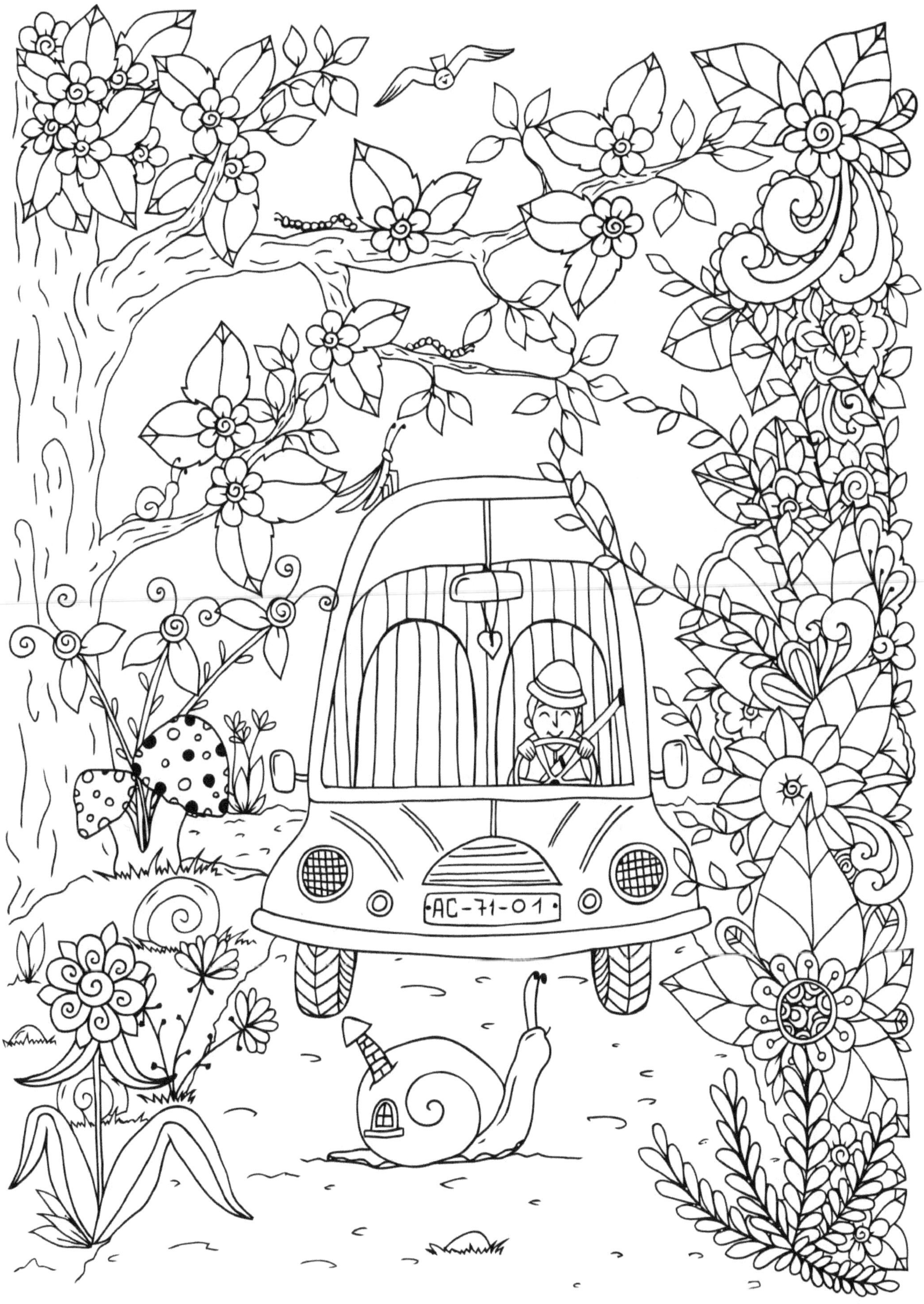
AC-71-01

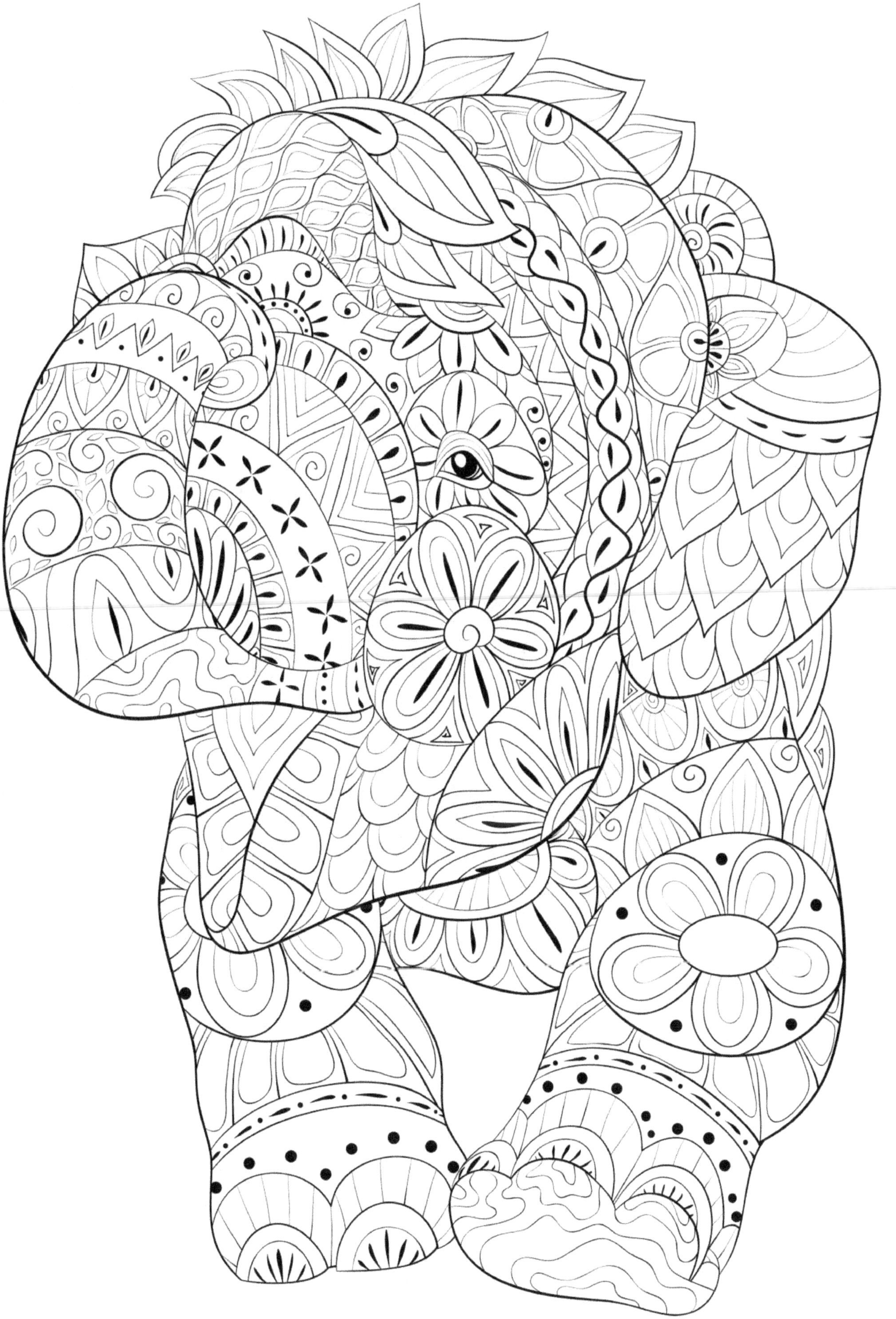

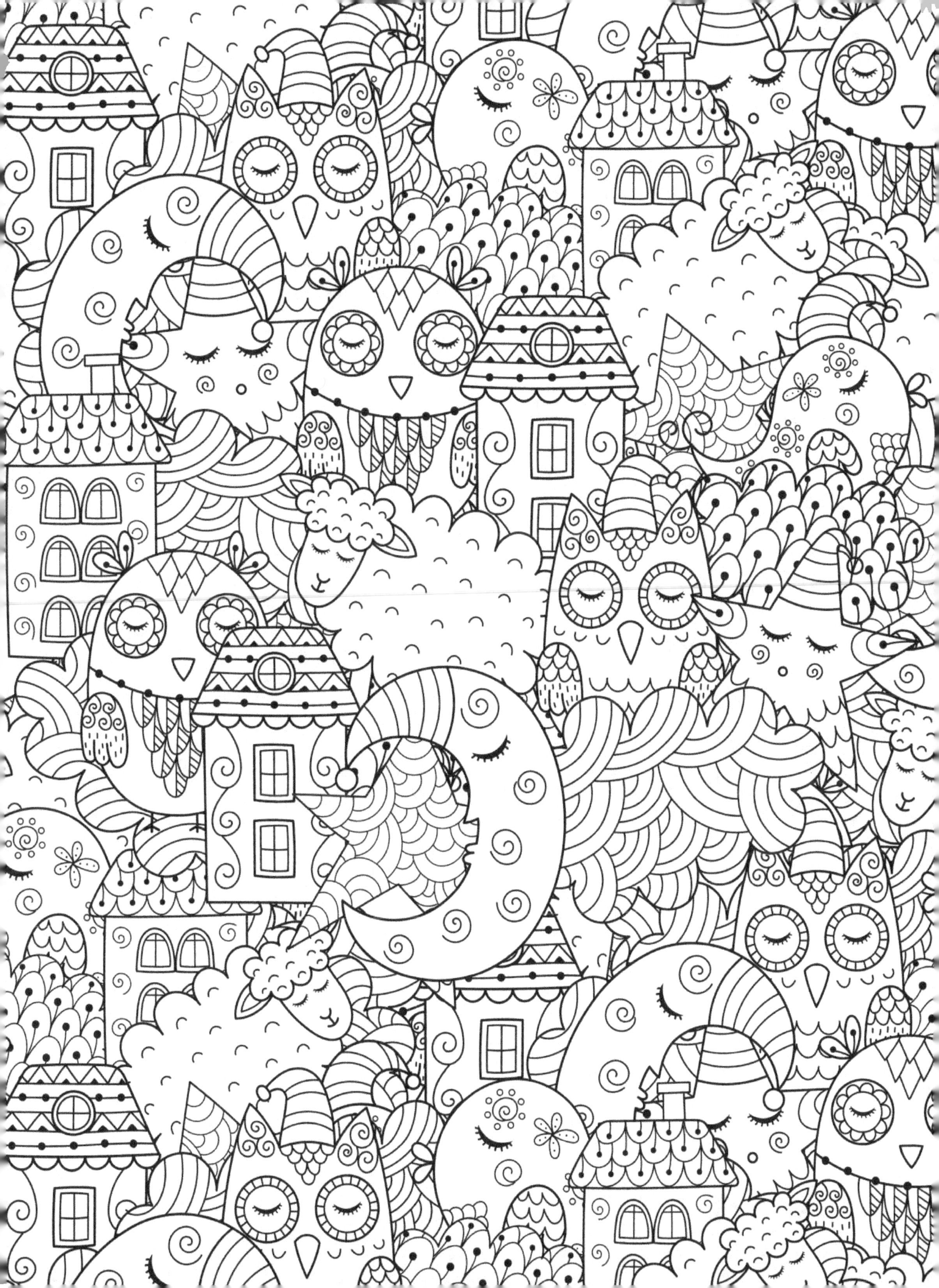

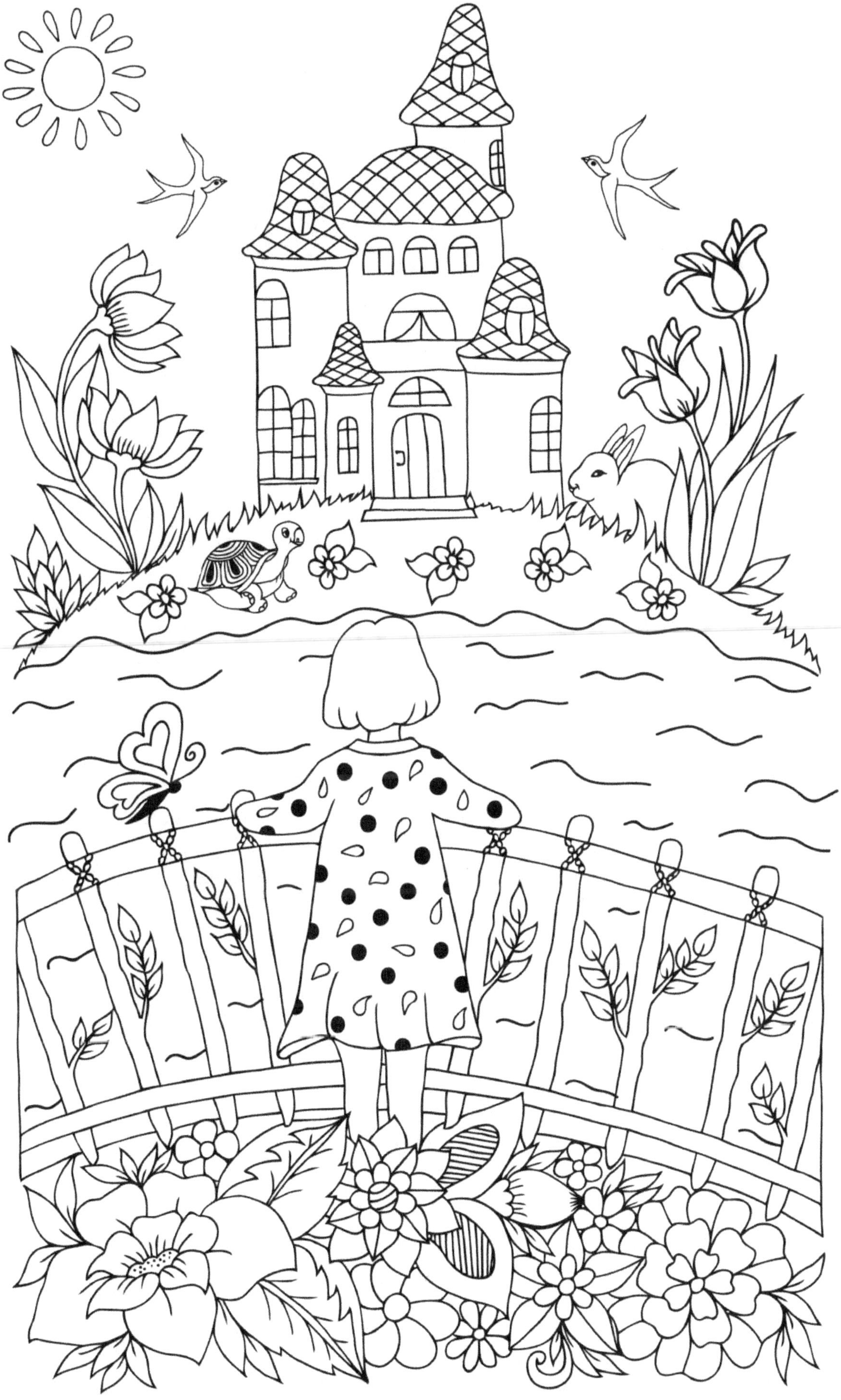

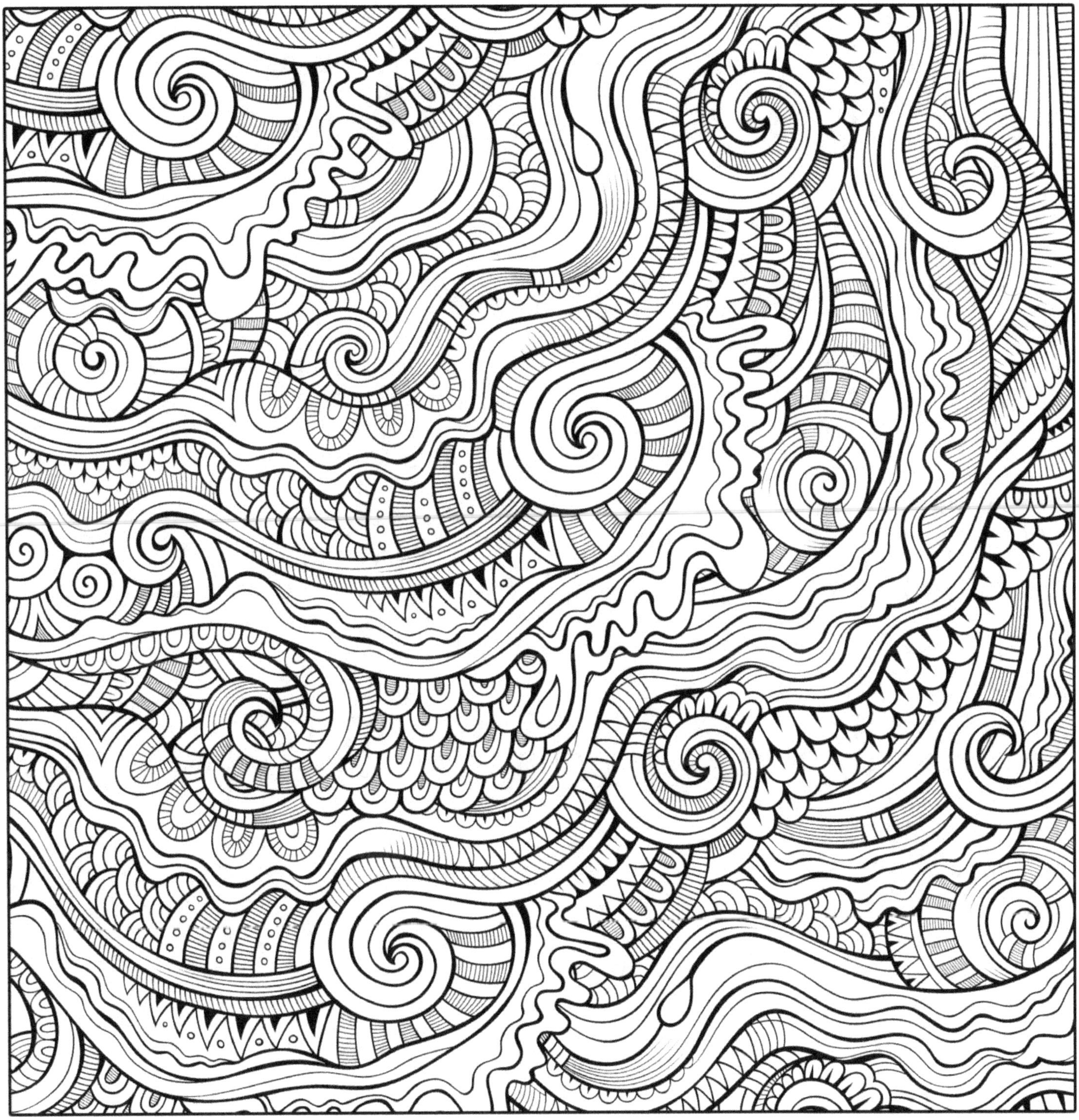

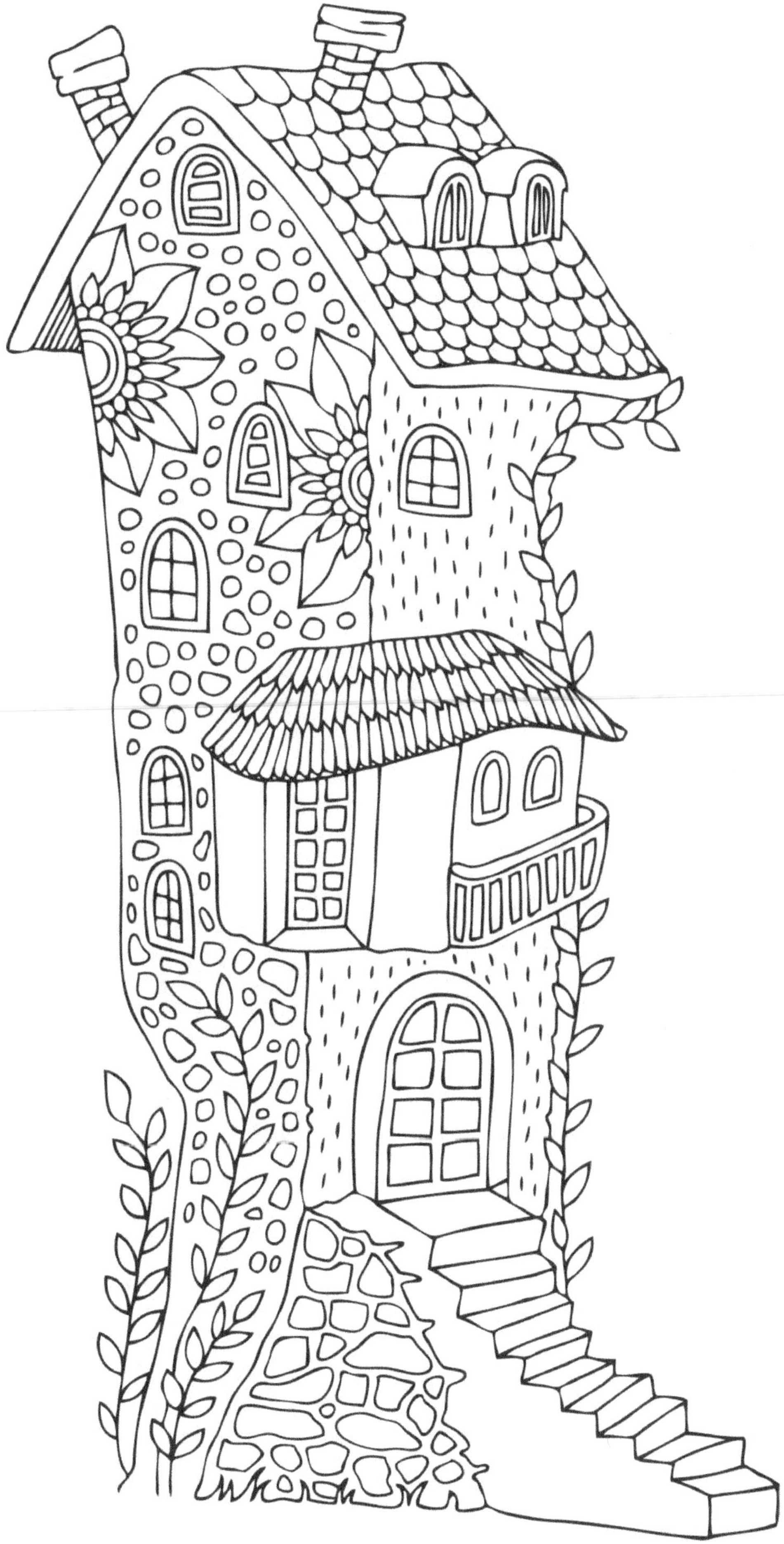

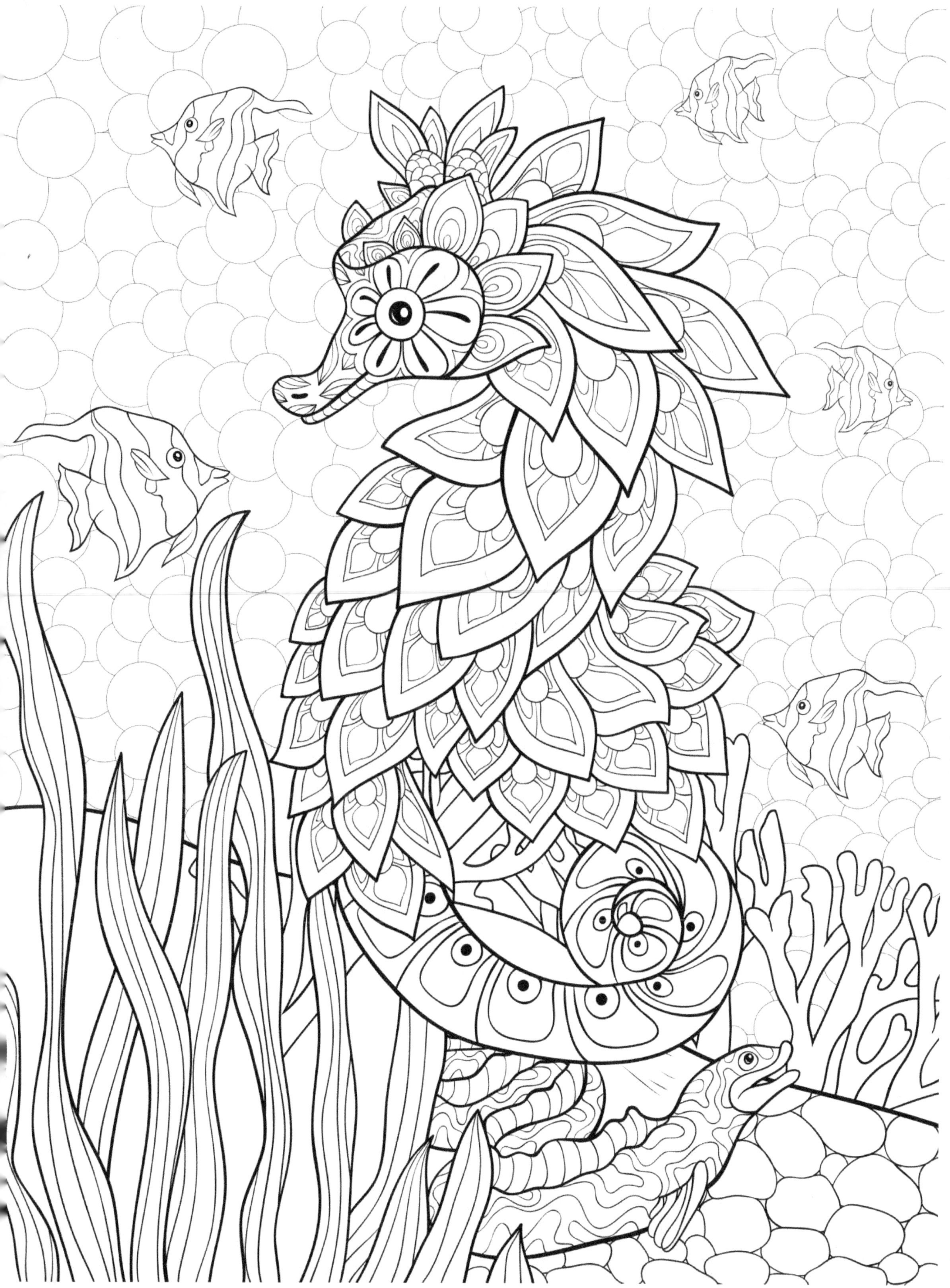

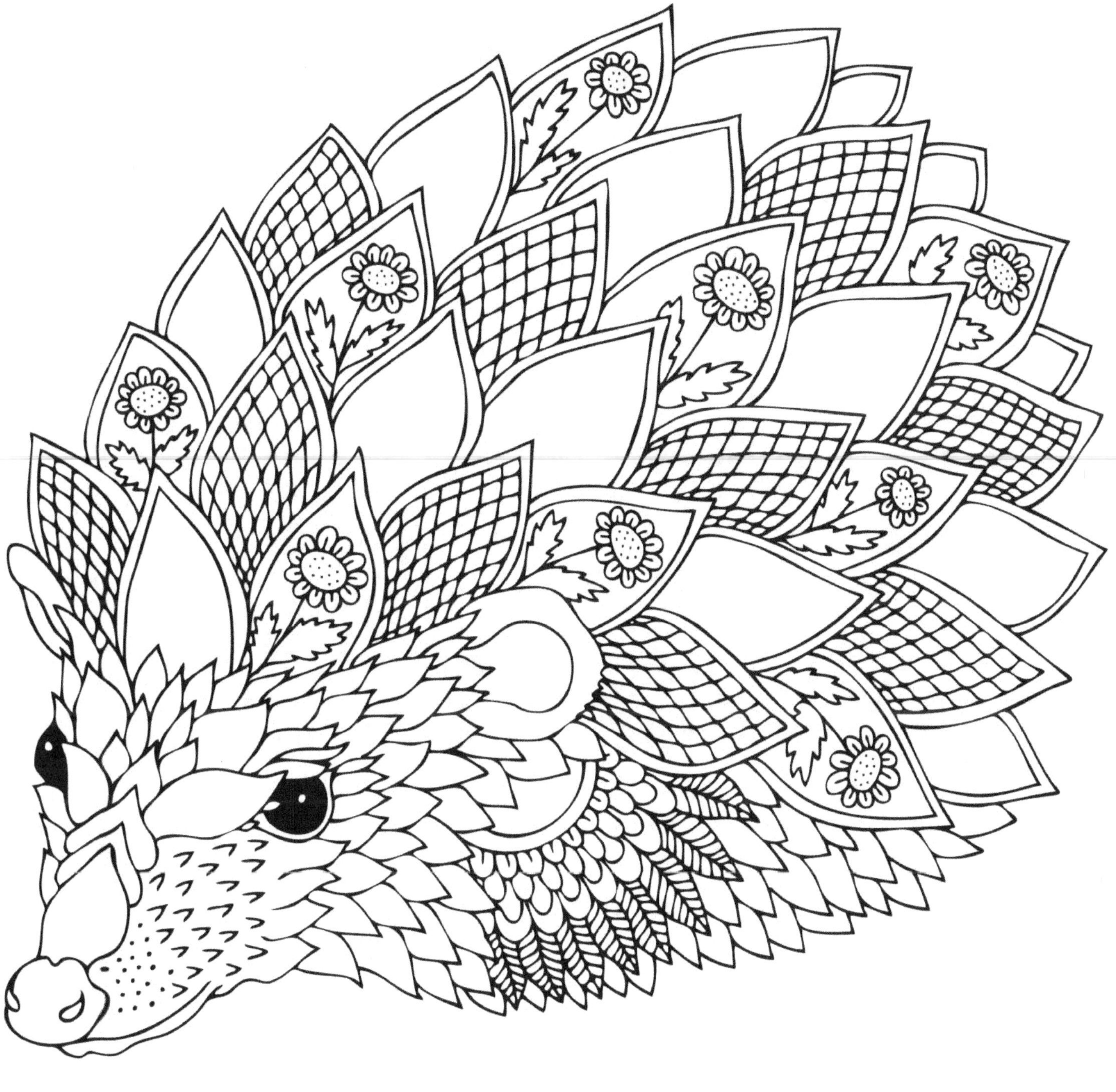

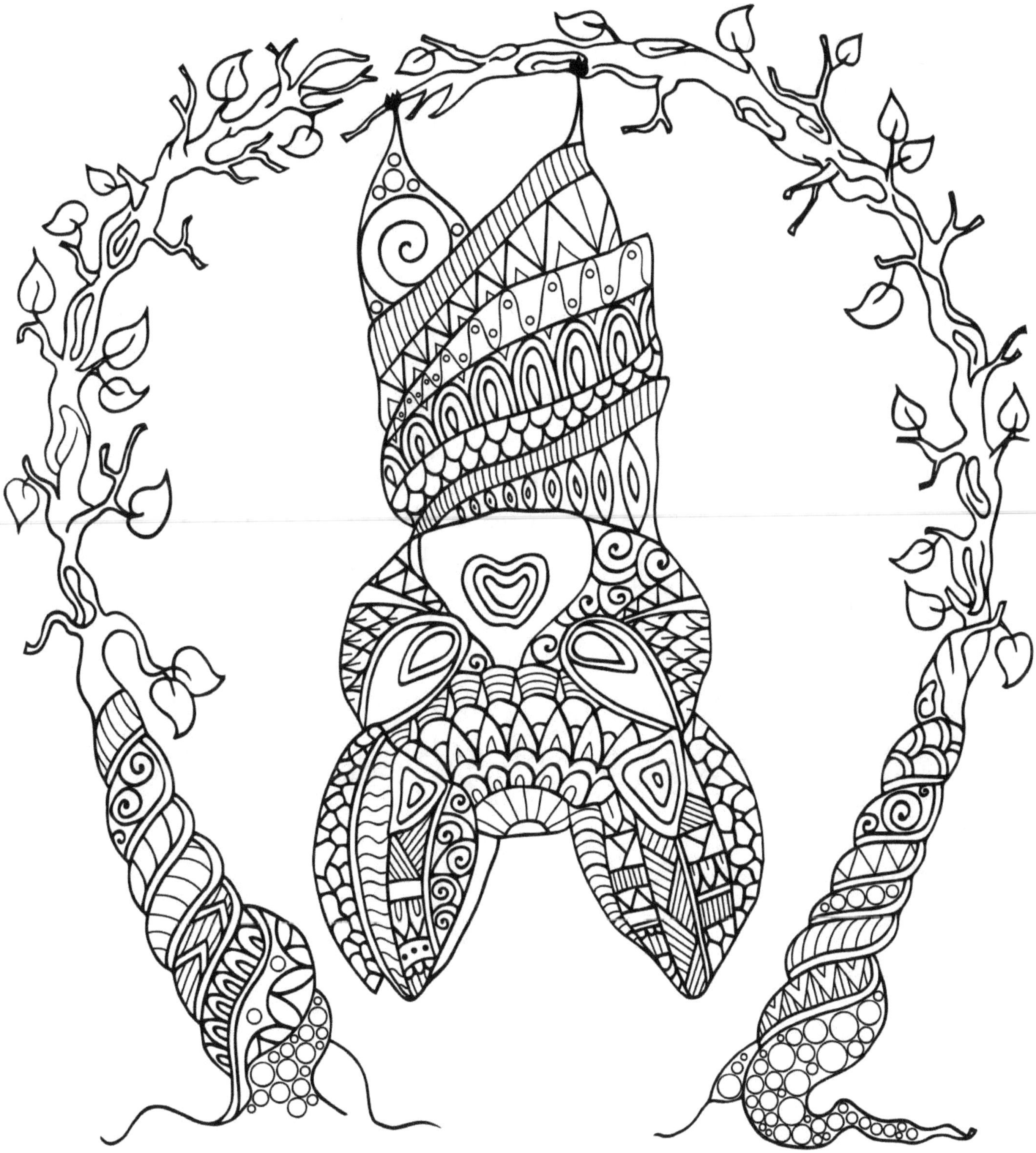

www.ingramcontent.com/pod-product-compliance
Lightning Source LLC
Chambersburg PA
CBHW062220220526
45471CB00009B/3277